FAN THE FLAME

FAN THE FLAME

Meditations for Spiritual Direction

ROB DES COTES

CLEMENTS PUBLISHING
Toronto

Fan the Flame
Copyright © 2006 by Rob Des Cotes
All rights reserved.

Published 2006 by Clements Publishing
6021 Yonge Street, Box 213
Toronto, Ontario M2M 3W2 Canada
www.clementspublishing.com

Unless otherwise noted, all Scripture quotations are from the
HOLY BIBLE, NEW INTERNATIONAL VERSION
copyright © 1973, 1978, 1984 by the International Bible Society.

Cover design by Rob Clements

Library and Archives Canada Cataloguing in Publication

Des Cotes, Rob, 1954-
Fan the flame : meditations for spiritual direction /
Rob Des Cotes.

ISBN 1-894667-83-2

1. Bible—Meditations. 2. Spiritual direction—Meditations.
I. Title.

BS491.5.D48 2006   242'.5
C2006-900251-7

CONTENTS

INTRODUCTION

The Bible, as we know, is multi-faceted. It reveals different glories according to the angle from which we approach it. Those who work for social justice find a great foundation for their hermeneutics in Scripture that others often never recognize. Persecuted communities find solace in its pages that others have no present need for. Evangelists, teachers and mentors find all they need there to be equipped in the particular work of the Gospel they are called to.

So too for contemplatives. People who have their hearts set on pilgrimage uncover unique insights in Scripture that provide spiritual direction for the journey of transformation they are on. The pages of the Bible are full of direct and indirect teachings on the nature of prayer and of the soul. Scriptures related to the contemplative life are often overlooked by those who read the Bible with other equally important objectives in mind. God, who is most capable of being all things to all people, seems to reveal to us the truth of whatever our hearts seek in the Scriptures.

The practice of prayer, especially one that recognizes the contemplative element, provides a perspective from which Scripture both reveals and confirms many signposts along the way. It is an interpretative guide that helps us make sense of the process of unknowing that leads to a growing encounter with God in our lives.

These meditations were first written as weekly encouragements for Imago Dei, a network of small faith communities around the world <www.imagodeicommunity.ca>. Members of these communities have found them helpful for promoting discussions on the practicalities of living the spiritual life. We would encourage you as well to consider reading and discussing these in a group along with other seekers.

Rob Des Cotes
March 21, 2006
Vancouver, B.C.

MEDITATIONS FOR SPIRITUAL DIRECTION

1

From one man He made every nation, that they should inhabit the whole earth; and He determined the times set for them and the exact places where they should live. God did this so that we would seek Him and perhaps reach out for Him and find Him, though He is not far from each one of us.

Acts 17:26-28

According to this passage we were created for the express purpose of seeking God, in the hope that we might "reach out for him, and find him." It's what most delights the Lord and it is also what leads to our own greatest glory.

To seek God is an honour bestowed by grace on the children of God. As Proverbs 25:2 says *"It is the glory of God to conceal a matter; to search out a matter is the glory of kings (and queens)."* The Lord appears to hide Himself in order that we may seek Him as our love grows. Elsewhere in Proverbs, God speaks of His pleasure in this exercise: *"I love those who love me, and those who seek me find me"* (Prov. 8:17).

The Lord extends His invitation to each one of us to daily seek His presence. And His assurance is that we will surely find Him if we do. Let us grow in our longing and our desire for God, for this is the very evidence of the Holy Spirit's presence within us. And as we continue to "reach out for Him," the Lord promises that He will refine and increase the capacity of our hearts to find Him.

> *You will seek me and find me when you seek me with all your heart.*
>
> Jeremiah 29:13

2

> *Foxes have holes and birds of the air have nests, but the Son of Man has no place to lay his head*
>
> Matthew 8:20

I used to feel sorry for Jesus whenever I read this passage. It reminded me of His birth narrative. For the Lord to still find "no room at the inn" seemed like a cruel expression of our inhospitality. But the more God is teaching me about the walk of faith the more I see this passage as a signpost of growth for anyone who would follow after Christ.

Jesus spoke these words to a teacher of the law who declared confidently "I will follow you wherever you go." The man was assuming they were heading for some earthly destination. Jesus' reply seems to say, "If you are going to follow me, you'll have to get used to being in a perpetual state of God-movement."

Something I read recently from Francois Fénelon, a 17th-century spiritual director, seems to confirm this experience. "Faith," he writes, "often holds the soul in a state of continued suspense, never quite able to touch a foot to solid ground."

Faith keeps us constantly up in the air, never quite certain what is going to happen next. In faith, we are willing to let God act with the most perfect freedom, without demands imposed by our expectations. We are fully resigned to His purpose in all things.

Fénelon refers to this type of faith as a "martyrdom of trust that takes place silently and without a stir." I know many people who would prefer to trust their foxholes. But for those who are called to exercise the mustard seed of faith they have, such words are helpful signposts that affirm the path we are on.

3

But small is the gate and narrow the road that leads to life, and only a few find it.

Matthew 7:15

I have been thinking lately about the cross and how it represents the entrance into the narrow way of life. It's a place where you instinctively become very small. As I imagine myself standing before it I always feel undone before the truth of what it represents. And I sense that God loves the healing that this undoing produces in us.

When we recognize the implications of Jesus' words, *"It is finished,"* we know that we no longer have any need nor reason to hold on to anything of ourselves. There is nothing we can do but give ourselves reciprocally to Christ, who has given all to us. This, according to Paul, is the only reasonable response if we truly recognize the significance of this act (Rom 12:1). There is nothing to do, nothing to hold onto—and this is good news.

God has shown me how too much of my spirituality is spent trying to "do myself up." While I am busy trying to pull myself together, I am actually working against the power of the cross which purposes to keep me undone in the presence of God. In the mystery of spiritual direction, the grace I receive while my life lies open and vulnerable at the foot of the cross is the very wholeness I seek. God's grace is truly sufficient, and is most evident in my weakness.

It's only as we learn how to remain undone at the foot of the cross that we will ever come to appreciate, first-hand, the all-sufficiency of God's grace.

Humble thyself in the sight of the Lord and He will lift you up.

James 4:10

4

A time to embrace and a time to refrain.

Ecclesiastes 3:6

This verse can be applied to two very different experiences of faith. There are seasons in life when faith is mostly a matter of waiting. It takes faith to trust God when you are anxious for something to happen, especially when you know He is calling you to abandon yourself to His will rather than covet what you hope for. This is a time to refrain from embracing.

The other side of faith shows up when it is time to act. This faith again requires trust, but it now gets applied to the courage to move. It calls not for passivity, but for the type of abandonment kayakers must feel when they launch into the white water and know the true meaning of the word commitment! This is a time to fully embrace the unknown.

May God give us discerning hearts to know which faith He is calling us to at different times.

5

Therefore do not worry about tomorrow, for tomorrow will worry about itself

Matthew 6:34

What is your relationship to the present? I think I used to be far more future-oriented than I am these days. My mind was always active, scanning the horizon of my life for new possibilities. I was seeking God's will but, instead of looking for it today, I was picturing it in the future and trying to adjust my day according to whatever I imagined to be coming from God. I've come to appreciate Paul's reminder that "No eye has seen, no ear has heard, no mind has conceived what God has prepared for those who love him" (1 Cor. 2:9). These days I tell myself that, if I've imagined it possible, it's probably not what God has in mind.

I'm **trying** to stop second-guessing God so that He can surprise me more.

> *Now to him who is able to do immeasurably more than all we ask or imagine, according to his power that is at work within us, to him be glory in the church and in Christ Jesus throughout all generations, for ever and ever! Amen.*
>
> Ephesians 3:20

6

> *Put on the new self, which is being renewed in knowledge in the image of its Creator.*
>
> Colossians 3:10

I love the wording of this verse, how it speaks of both the active and passive experience of spiritual growth. Paul tells us that we are to "put on the new self." The verb tense here is continual, meaning it is not a once-for-all action but an ongoing, every day, every minute act of reaching up to heaven for that which is freshly born from above.

But Paul also defines this new self as that which is being constantly renewed, re-created directly by the hand of God. It receives its definition, its spiritual direction, and its image according to the likeness of its Creator, whose mercies are revealed every minute of our lives.

As we look to God for fresh manna—the daily bread of who we are—we are cautioned about the short shelf life of the images we carry. They are not meant to be stored for tomorrow. Why live with the memory of what God's presence was yesterday when we can reach afresh for the reality of Christ's light in this moment?

Paul tells us that we must be continually active in putting on the new self so that the Lord, who is the Way, the Truth and the Life of all we are becoming can continually renew His image within us.

7

. . . only one thing is needed. Mary has chosen what is better.

Luke 10:42

Like all of us I find the concept of the "flesh at war with the spirit" most apparent when it comes to settling down to prayer. As Martha would agree, prayer is only one among a whole list of important things that need to be done in a day.

And yet, when I am in prayer, I often sense Jesus chiding me about what He has been trying to tell me through those many tugs He gives my heart each day—"only one thing is needed."

In those moments He tells me that I have chosen what is better and He assures me, as He did Mary, that "it will not be taken away" from my day's work.

8

I always do what pleases the Father.

John 8:29

Moment by moment, God's will expresses itself upon each one of us. As we seek to be attentive and conformed to it, we not only discover the living activity of God in our lives, but we also discover the truth of who we are called to be. It brings great joy in heaven whenever we are free to truly be who we are—God's will expressed on earth.

Seeking to be whatever God's will is in our day implies an ongoing fellowship with Him. It requires a disposition towards obedience and a constant readiness to be re-directed by God, whose ways are always greater than ours. A growing attentiveness to God, as an expression of our servant-love, will cause us to increase in the direction of unceasing prayer. The best motivation for this discipline is simply to seek, as Jesus did, to please the Father always.

Let us listen to what God inspires in us. Let us test the spirit that is moving in us, to see if it comes from God. And after we have recognized God, let us stop at nothing to please Him.

—Francois Fénelon

9

In all your ways acknowledge Him, and He will make your paths straight.

Proverbs 3:6

If anyone is looking for a straight path in life there appears to be a foolproof way to avoid all the zigzags. For any of us who are tired of watching our crooked buildings collapse there is word of a true plumb line from which we can always build anew—acknowledge Him in all your ways.

Report back to God often in your day, come to Him for correction, for confirmation of what you think He is saying, and with a readiness to always have your path redirected. And the promise is that He will direct your ways as surely as if He were walking them Himself. What good news this is for anyone who would choose to be so child-like as to continually check in with their parent.

God is calling us to a new parent-child relationship—not one that comes from the expectation of the parent, but one that comes from the child who enjoys the security of knowing the Father agrees with all they do.

How easy it is for God to lead those who constantly look to Him for guidance. If we acknowledge Him in all our ways, we will surely walk the path that leads to life.

10

I will give them an undivided heart and put a new spirit in them; I will remove from them their heart of stone and give them

a heart of flesh. Then they will follow my decrees and be carefu...
to keep my laws.

Ezekiel 11:19

What a true description of the spiritual direction we experien.. as our hearts "melt" in the presence of God. Every day, as each hour passes by, there is an ebb and flow in the condition of our hearts. Ezekiel's insight truly describes the poles between which we fluctuate—between a heart of stone and a heart of flesh.

My heart of stone is tight, guarded, self-controlled and unresponsive to God and to others. My heart of flesh however is soft, easily led by the gentle touch of the Spirit, and sensitively responsive to God's leading in all my relationships. To experience the restoration of our hearts is a gift of salvation. None of us can recover this on our own. But Jesus, in making all things new, can and does restore our hearts to a state of sensitivity to the divine impulse.

Consider how these states of heart apply to you. What are the factors that contribute to the hardening or softening of your heart? Let us present ourselves often to Christ for the restoration of our souls. Mountains melt like wax before the Lord. Surely our hearts do as well.

11

In repentance and rest is your salvation, in quietness and trust
is your strength.

Isaiah 30:15

I thought I heard God answer me this week in response to my question, "Lord, how can I walk more consistently in your Presence?" He said, "Stay small, and slow."

If one of the ways we discern whether a spirit is from God is by the fruit it bears, I would say that the tempering effect this little piece of advice has had on my week is a good indicator that this word has begun to accomplish the purpose for which it was sent. I believe it is a good word for anyone who wishes to remain attentive to God throughout their day.

David
#12

he things that most often pull me away from the center of my
tionship with God have always been my presuming greater autonomy,
re control, and a faster pace in my life than is true of His calling. I often
e giant steps and assume much more responsibility than is appropriate
someone who is trying to live a life of God-directed faith.

"Stay small and slow." Small—in the direction of the mustard seed that
bears the greatest fruit; and slow—in the direction of the stillness that
truly knows God. Practice these, remaining in God's love, and Jesus says
we will bear much fruit.

Small—the fruit of humility

Slow—the fruit of tranquil, trusting, faith.

12

The body is made up of many parts . . . . the eye cannot say to
the hand, I don't need you . . . On the contrary, those parts of the
body that seem to be weaker are indispensable.

1 Corinthians 12:14-23

We know that Paul wrote this in reference to the variety of individual
gifts we find among us in the body of Christ. But this same
passage is helpful when we consider it in terms of spiritual direction—as
it applies to the many 'parts' we discover within ourselves as we grow in
self-knowledge. We can easily be tempted to assume for ourselves the task
of separating the weeds from the wheat. We are clearly told however that
this is surgeon's work that is best left to Jesus (Matt. 13:29). But what do
we do in the meantime with all the good, bad and ugly truth we discover
within ourselves?

Since adolescence, most of my inner struggles have had to do with
trying to create a whole out of the many discrepancies I find within
myself. I have often been discouraged by my inability to be consistent
in who I am. Many aspects within me seem to contradict each other as
they negate the truth of who I think I am. For years I convinced myself
that this was just a passing phase—that I would eventually get rid of the
inconsistent elements of my personality and get on with being who I
really am.

After over 50 years of trying, I've come to accept that I'm no more consistent than ever at being who I am. If anything I seem to be less so. Like all of us, I am a kaleidoscope of personalities—I am wise, I am foolish; sometimes a saint, more often a sinner; I am strong, I am weak; I am good, I am evil; I love and I don't love; I act appropriately, I act inappropriately; I am courageous, yet I am full of fears; I find myself often in the very presence of God and yet, most of the time, I feel hopelessly lost. And I can be all these things in just one day!

If we are to grow in the truth of self-knowledge we have to accept that we really are all the things that take place within us. Through faith in Christ's love we need to learn how to accept the many personalities that make up our life.

The advice that St. Frances de Sales gave his directees was to "grow familiar with your burden, as if you and it were to always live together." Self-understanding can only grow according to our self-acceptance. It will lead us, through humility, to the truth of who we are.

Paul gave himself the mandate to be all things to all people. I need to learn to give myself permission to be all things to myself—and to trust God to separate the weeds from the wheat.

13

Therefore keep watch, because you do not know the day or the hour.

Matthew 25:13

The person who prays grows in their capacity to recognize and accept life as mystery, that its ways are largely unknown. We need to accept this limitation as God-ordained and to detach ourselves from our compulsive need to understand (i.e. to control) life.

Detachment represents a spiritual freedom that is only possible when your life is no longer constrained by your preconceptions. It's easy to imagine the growth opportunities this gives our Creator. Any artist knows the creative freedom that happens once they let go of their preconceptions.

Detachment is a gentle and delicate act. It's a state of relaxed expectancy that leans forward into the mystery of whatever God might do next. It is a patient and trusting disposition and it inevitably leads to waiting—longing and anticipating in the hope of what is coming.

Like all forms of detachment, waiting means to humbly let go of control—in most cases the control of time and outcome. It naturally produces anxiety in us. But, as we grow in the grace of waiting, it leads to an open-handedness where we no longer cling to our expectations of what or how we will receive from God. As Richard Rohr puts it, "when we live out of ego, we impose our demands on reality. But when we live in God's presence, we await reality's demands on us."

Waiting on God is the posture that requires the most faith from us. It's no wonder the Lord loves it so.

My soul waits only upon God, for all my expectations are from him.

Psalm 62:1

14

Devote yourselves to prayer, being watchful and thankful.

Colossians 4:2

It's hard to keep watch. In such a variety of ways we end up falling asleep. One of the ways we do so is by closing our minds and no longer "seeing" what we were looking at. We shut down what we have been observing and turn it into something we think we know and now no longer have to watch.

The moment I think I have understood something, I no longer watch it in the same way as when I was trying to discover what was going on. The moment I pass judgment on something, I am no longer impartially observing the nuances of its unfolding. The moment my will engages in order to influence something in the direction I think it should go, I am no longer able to watch closely in order to discover where God is taking it. These are only a few of the ways I fall asleep.

It is difficult to stay alert. It requires a particular type of wisdom, the type James describes as pure, coming from above (James 3:17). It is pure because it is impartial, gentle. It doesn't leave its own footprint on the unfolding of life by either imposing itself or by shutting down an experience prematurely.

Once we think we know what God is doing we no longer need God. We can now follow the image we are picturing. And that's the idol our Living God wishes to free us from. To stay awake means learning how to keep our eyes open to the new thing God is doing every moment of our lives.

Praise with elation, praise every morning,
God's re-creation of the new day.

15

Take no thought of tomorrow, there is enough for today.
Matthew 6:34

There is only one life happening, and that's God's life which He creates and sustains, moment by moment. The purpose of our prayer is to help us find God each day as the One who gives us life. Perhaps one of the reasons we have such difficulty finding our life in God is that we don't accept the life He gives us. We often seem to be looking elsewhere for it, mostly in our own imaginations.

Our minds, it seems, are not primarily designed for the moment. If yours is anything like mine, it's usually pretty active in the day, scanning the horizons of life, looking for alternative options or other possible futures than the one I'm living now. My mind is very other-than-now oriented. And when it's not looking ahead, it's just as busy minding the past. Our thoughts are just not designed to stay focused on the present for very long.

Our hearts, on the other hand, seem created to receive and embrace the life that is happening here and now. If we are to grow towards accepting life as it really is, it is the heart that will most likely lead the relationship.

In order to simply accept the life that God is giving me, I need to stop looking over the fence, envying or pining for some other life. It sounds so easy doesn't it? We need to be grateful to our minds for doing such an excellent job of researching other possibilities for us. But let's also assure them that there is a pretty good life going on right here and now, and that we can be quite happy to rest in it as it is.

Albert Hasse, a contemporary writer on prayer said, "the present moment is the appointed place for meeting God." This is the only day the Lord has made, let us rejoice and be glad in it!

16

For we are God's workmanship, created in Christ Jesus to do
good works, which God prepared in advance for us to do.

Ephesians 2:10

This word speaks of our vocation. It reminds us that the goal of spiritual direction is not knowledge but action which, in Christ Jesus, God prepared in advance for us to do. As we discover our "name in Christ" we find that our name is, in fact, a "good work"—a particular expression of God's will that He fulfills in and through us. We find that being and doing increasingly become the same thing.

Our vocation, our name in Christ, is something that God calls forth. It's not the type of job description that we can choose beforehand and then set out to accomplish. It's one that we realize as we go, almost after the fact. As we respond more fully to God's calling, our vocation becomes revealed to us as more of a gift than as our own creation or offering.

The Lord calls, equips and sets us up to do the works that He prepared in advance for us to do. It is a free gift of grace. And, in each life given to Christ, God sees this work as good.

If we remain centered in Christ, bearing the fruit He promised, we will have a wonderful ringside seat from which to observe God's work unfolding in us. Our job then is simply to praise Him for His—for His good workmanship in us as we agree with Him that "it is good."

Be open each day to receive God's grace in whatever He calls you to do. And watch for signs of Paul's assurance of this grace abounding all around you. As he writes in 2 Corinthians 9:8:

God is able to make all grace abound to you, so that in all things, at all times, having all that you need, you will abound in every good work.

17

Therefore, I urge you, brothers and sisters, in view of God's mercy, to offer your bodies as living sacrifices, holy and pleasing to God—this is your spiritual act of worship.

Romans 12:1

During prayer I found myself asking the Lord, "What is best for me to be doing when I pray? What is most profitable to spiritual growth?" I was reminded of Paul's instructions that our most complete offering is to present ourselves as "living sacrifices." If my desire is that God dwell more fully in me, this seems like a reasonable first step. It's the only way I can ever hope to claim the identity that Paul had for himself when he wrote: "it is no longer I who live, but Christ who lives in me." (Gal. 2:20)

Contemplative prayer is an offering whereby we place ourselves on the altar of spiritual formation and let God create in us whatever is needed. We sacrifice our right to self-will and determination in deference to the Lord's will and determination. As a living sacrifice my prayer is simply to present myself daily to the Holy Spirit. Once I put my life on this altar, it is no longer mine but His, to do with as He pleases.

According to Paul, God recognizes such a life of self-offering as "holy and pleasing." This was the relationship with the Father that Jesus modeled while He was on earth, and which He calls us to imitate in our relationship with Him. As we continually offer our lives as a sacrifice to God, we will surely grow in the experience of Christ, who lives in us.

18

Blessed are the poor in spirit for theirs is the kingdom of heaven.

Matthew 5:3

In the *Dark Night of the Soul,* St. John of the Cross encourages us to "make perfect the inner poverty of spirit."

St. John teaches that, as we approach God in our journey, we inevitably enter a realm of mystery where we recognize that we are no longer in a position to lay down the terms and conditions of the relationship. In order to progress in the spiritual life we must lose our sense of mastery and control over it, our sense of being able to deal with God on our own terms. In so doing, we move beyond our own version of reality—one that is largely self-constructed—and more towards truth as God defines and reveals it to us.

As we walk along a path that is no longer self-determined we are stripped of all guarantees which are rooted in our selves. We begin to truly live a life of faith, love, and trust in God as the sole Author and Finisher of our faith. It's no wonder that this undoing presents us with such difficulties. St. John of the Cross teaches that such growth will naturally be accompanied by a sense of loss which will lead us to experience the true poverty of spirit that Jesus is referring to here.

In the paradox of faith, when you feel that you've lost your sense of competence in your spiritual life it could well be a sign of real spiritual progress in the direction of a deeper dependence on God. An awareness of inner poverty, of having nothing of your own to offer God, should be cause for peace rather than disturbance since it is, in Jesus' teaching, the very condition that ushers in blessing.

19

O LORD, our God, other lords besides You have ruled over us, but Your name alone do we honour. They are now dead, they live no more.

Isaiah 26:12-14

G regory of Nissa (4th century) saw the story of the Exodus as a metaphor of our being freed from the "other lords that have ruled over us" As the Israelites fled, the Egyptians pursued them as far as the Red Sea. They found themselves, quite literally, at a dead end. The sea represented the limits of their own resources. Without God's intervention this was as far away as they could get from their oppressors.

Suddenly, the sea opened up and the Israelites were encouraged to enter into the unexpected path that God had prepared for their salvation. But the Egyptians followed after them. Little did they know that the path of salvation was designed only for those who were being redeemed. It's a highway which Isaiah calls Holiness,

> *The unclean will not journey on it; it will be for those who walk*
> *in that Way; wicked fools will not go about on it.*
>
> Isaiah 35:7-9

The Egyptians took occasion to follow therein, not realizing the trap that had been set for them. In the same way that Jesus tricked the devil into following Him into death, the slave masters, by trying to reclaim the Israelites, were lured to their destruction.

Gregory of Nissa draws attention to the fact that the same path that God lays out as the means to spiritual freedom also brings death to the forces that enslave us. The sea, or our spiritual direction, represents both that which leads us to God as well as that which ultimately separates us from our sins.

Though our sins continue to pursue us, often nipping at our heels, the sea, at God's initiative, will one day close on them. Looking behind us, we too will say "they are now dead, they live no more." As we faithfully await our salvation, Isaiah assures us:

> *In that day they will say, "Surely this is our God; we trusted in*
> *Him and He saved us. This is the Lord, we trusted in Him; Let*
> *us rejoice and be glad in His salvation.*
>
> Isaiah 25:9

20

Whoever finds his life will lose it, and whoever loses his life for my sake will find it.

Matthew 11:39

Each of the gospels repeat this important teaching that Jesus gave. In a variety of ways the Lord is trying to make us understand something crucial . . . "The one who loves their life will lose it, while the one who hates their life in this world will keep it for eternal life. . . . If anyone would come after me, he must deny himself. . . . Any of you who does not give up everything he has cannot be my disciple."

The same Jesus who came to give us a more abundant life cautions us about holding on too tightly to the one we have. Rather than love our lives directly, we are to let go and look beyond them, in order to follow more closely the Giver of life.

In what ways might your relationship to life be obstructing your relationship to God? What would it mean for you to "lose your life" in order to find it in Christ? These are the questions that need to be asked if we're going to experience the truth of one of Jesus' more difficult sayings.

The Lord invites us to examine our lives in light of this teaching and to explore for ourselves the paradoxical wisdom by which He leads us to greater Truth.

To advance spiritually we must be still . . . to grow we must become small. . . to accumulate we must let go . . . to have perfect freedom we must perfectly submit our wills to God . . . to gain life we must learn how to continually lose it.

Welcome to the kingdom of God. It's not what you'd expect.

21

. . . Anyone who comes to Him must believe that He exists and that He rewards those who earnestly seek Him.

Hebrews 11:6

To love God and to know the truth of what is: that is my intention every time I sit down to pray. It's what I have to keep reminding myself of as my thoughts flit about over many distractions. This intention is what reels me in from all the other concerns I have and focuses me towards the goal I choose as my first pursuit in life.

To know the truth of "what is" means I have to stop thinking about what is and learn to look directly at it. I can only really observe what is from the stillness of Truth. Whenever my spirit is still, I am struck by the awesome simplicity of life—how nothing is really happening except for God. From that place of prayer I know with certainty that He is truly "all in all," and that to love Him wholly is what we were made for.

In contemplative prayer I am often led to that secret place, somewhere below the waves of life, where the only movement taking place is that of the Holy Spirit and my soul loving each other. It's in that precious place that, once again, we have insight into what eternity means.

22

. . . anyone who comes to Him must believe that He exists.
Hebrews 11:6

The realm of God exists in my life and I have opportunity, as I desire to seek it, to grow in the knowledge and experience of eternity. Having tasted this, even once, I am ruined for anything less in life. The Franciscan monk, Richard Rohr, wrote that,

> True contemplation looks for the place of perfect simplicity. You can't stay there, but if you know this simplicity once, it is enough for a whole lifetime. You know your life is radically okay. That you are a child of God. You are in union. There is nothing to prove, nothing to attain. Everything is already there.

That God rewards those who earnestly seek Him is the testimony we bear witness of in this world. If Christians are to be true light in the darkness we need to be among those who are most eager to seek and find that light each day.

The world should see Christians as the chief seekers of truth—those who lead the pursuit because we are so convinced that God is to be found by those who earnestly seek Him.

How much more winsome would this be—to be known as seekers—than to present ourselves to the world as those who have "found it." The zeal and passion with which we pursue Truth, as well as the love of God we discover in the process of transformation, will resonate much more deeply in those who are hungry for God than any other apologetics we will ever come up with.

23

Jesus said, "Peace be with you! As the Father has sent me, I am sending you." And with that he breathed on them and said, "Receive the Holy Spirit."

John 20:21

I met with my spiritual director last week. In the course of our time together we examined the mystery of how we participate most with our spiritual growth by simply being receptive to God. This is the age-old "to be or not to be" question to which prayer inevitably leads us. What part do I play in my spiritual life? What part does God play? And at what point does my own participation actually begin to hinder my spiritual growth?

In speaking of this matter, Jeanne Guyon, a 17th century Christian contemplative, used the metaphor of a ship that leaves the port. All the sailors are working hard, pulling at the oars in order to make the ship advance. But once the vessel is at sea and has found favourable winds, the pilot simply spreads the sails and holds the rudder. She writes,

> Oh what progress they make without becoming the least bit tired. They are making more progress in one hour without any effort than they ever did before, even when exerting all their strength. If the oars were used now, it would only slow the ship and cause fatigue . . . they are now useless and unnecessary.

Jesus' command to His disciples was to simply, "Receive the Holy Spirit." What is the life God is inviting you to receive, without effort, from Him?

I tell you the truth, anyone who will not receive the kingdom of God like a little child will never enter it.

Mark 10:15

24

I know, my God, that you test the heart and are pleased with integrity. All these things have I given willingly and with honest intent. And now I have seen with joy how willingly your people who are here have given to you. O LORD, God of our fathers Abraham, Isaac and Israel, keep this desire in the hearts of your people forever, and keep their hearts loyal to you.

1 Chronicles 29:17-18

My underlying belief about spiritual community is that, as we each remain enthusiastic about our individual spiritual direction and growth, and as we value the support of others in this, community will largely happen on its own. Community is the natural fruit of spiritual life that comes from the joy of being in an environment with others who are sincerely seeking God.

As I read David's words about his own community of faith I feel something of the joy he expresses to God of "how willingly your people who are here have given to you." We should rejoice as well at the faith of others. And pray, for the sake of such precious communities, that God preserves the integrity of those around us.

David recognized that God tests the hearts of those who seek Him and is pleased with such integrity. As seekers, our responsibility is to be honest with the intent of our hearts, and to be praying for each other as David did for his community, "O LORD, God of our fathers Abraham, Isaac and Israel, keep this desire in the hearts of your people forever, and keep their hearts loyal to you."

As we pray for one another in this way let us also work together to counter the many distractions and diversions that keep us from the one thing we desire most—a close and growing relationship with the real presence of God in our lives.

25

God is love. Whoever lives in love lives in God, and God in them.

1 John 4:16

Always precise in his theology, John doesn't simply say that God is loving or that God has love. He writes specifically that "God is love," which is the same as saying that "love is God."

Love is freedom. It softens the heart, it tickles the soul. It is fluid, alive. It is spacious and full of hope. Love is what we discover as we pray.

If you've ever felt love you have felt the presence of God. The living presence of love that we experience in ourselves and in others, and its noble qualities of sacrifice, generosity, forbearance, hospitality and compassion, are evidence of the very character of God within us.

When we think in these terms it is easy to discern God in our lives. If you are seeking God, simply seek love. If you want to follow God in your day, your leading question should be "where is love?" If we don't want to lose sight of God then, as Jesus taught us, we must first learn how to remain in His love. This is the only way to truly practice the presence of God.

26

Burnt offerings and sin offerings you did not require. Then I said, "Here I am, I have come.... I desire to do your will, O my God; your law is within my heart."

Psalm 40:6-8

It is easy to turn our relationship with God, especially our prayer relationship, into a method or a technique for self-improvement. But God has ordained that the door to intimacy remain closed to anyone who would try to enter by any other means than love. Our love for God reaches beyond the veil that encloses us. It alone can release us from the force of gravity that binds us to ourselves.

Dionysius the Areopagite spoke of a "dart of love" that we must throw outwards from ourselves towards God. Like a grappling hook it will pull us out of the confines of our self-orientation into the arms of God. There is no other way out of the closed system of self than to reach out, in love, to the Divine Other.

O Father, we thank You for relationship with Jesus Christ in whom we are poured out as a love offering. Receive us that we would be caught up in the movement of Your Spirit. Pull us upwards, towards the Love that is You.

27

Lord, teach us to pray.

Luke 11:1

The Lord responded to this request by teaching His disciples what we now call "the Lord's Prayer." Ever since, these words have become the central utterance of the historical church. They are words that we are meant to embody as our first concerns of life. It is a beautiful prayer to recite, but it is in living each of these petitions that the power of these words becomes rooted in our thoughts, attitudes, actions and desires. Through these words we line up our desires with those of our Lord.

I have longed to shape my life according to this prayer and have been helped by a simple format that might serve you as well. Whenever I have tried to meditate on the various petitions during a single prayer time I have always found it overwhelming. Each verse is a *lectio divina* of its own. But the Lord's Prayer can easily be walked through on a weekly basis, focusing on one meditation each day. A relationship with the Lord's Prayer over the course of a week could look like this:

Monday: *Our Father who art in heaven, hallowed be thy name...*

- consider today the many ways God nurtures us
- consider how the word "our" presumes a relationship with God that is a shared one
- meditate on the fact that, though God is with us and within us, He is also high above us. He is both immanent and transcendent

- consider your relationship to a God whose name is hallowed, holy

Tuesday: *Thy kingdom come, thy will be done on earth as it is in heaven...*

- meditate on the need for change in the world
- consider the difference it will make and desire the day when every person will know the Lord for themselves. (Jer. 31:34)
- rejoice at the hope of everything being as it should; imagine the unity of agreement between heaven and earth, and among all people

Wednesday: *Give us this day our daily bread...*

— it is half way through the week; pray for the conditions of your home or work place

— meditate on your circumstances, whether in need or in plenty, and consider all to be from God's hand

— give thanks to God for the needs you do have; see yourself among those who are blessed because you hunger God-ward.

Thursday: *Forgive us our trespasses...*

- the week now turns towards Sunday when you will once again meet the Lord in communion; it is time to "prepare the way of the Lord"
- spend time today taking stock of your life; confess all that represents a trespass of God's loving desire for your life
- consider the ways your life has either intentionally or inadvertently worked against God's purposes in you, and in your relationship with others
- be grateful for the confidence you have in asking for forgiveness, and for the assurance you have that you will receive it

Friday: *...as we forgive those who trespass against us...*

- Friday, in many Christian traditions, is considered a day of mercy since it was the day the Lord gave His life for us. As we have freely received mercy when we asked for it yesterday, today we consider all those who offend us as we pray for the faith to forgive them

- as Christ does for you, present others to yourself as 'spotless, without blemish' (Eph. 5:27)
- forgive yourself also, for all the ways you think you fail in your own eyes

Saturday: *And lead us not into temptation but deliver us from evil...*

- Saturday, in most Christian traditions, is seen as a day of waiting, as it lies between Good Friday and Resurrection Sunday
- in the days preceding, you have asked for and have received forgiveness. Jesus now says to us, "go and sin no more." Today is a day when you strive to remain in His love, clean because of the grace you have received from His hand
- let us not underestimate the daily help we need in order to continually walk in righteousness

Sunday: *For thine is the Kingdom, the power and the glory forever and ever, Amen.*

- the Lord's Day is a day of victory that affirms God's rule over sin and death
- we meditate on eternity, when God's glory will no longer be seen dimly, but will be fully recognized by all-rest in the confidence that God's sovereign power will achieve all that He has promised.
- rest in the confidence that God's sovereign power can and will achieve all that He has promised.

28

. . . who was declared with power to be the Son of God by his resurrection from the dead: Jesus Christ our Lord.

Romans 1:4b

It took the awesome power of the resurrection to declare, without ambiguity, that Jesus Christ was truly the Son of God. And it will likely take that same resurrection power to convince the principalities and powers that we too are truly what the Scriptures say we are—the sons and daughters of the Most High God.

Throughout His life the question of Jesus' identity was always being contested. The few who affirmed the truth of who He was were far outnumbered by the many who cast doubts and outrightly dismissed His claims. During Jesus' temptation in the desert the devil was not trying to take advantage of the Lord's fleshly weakness as much as openly challenging Jesus' self-identity: "...if You truly are the Son of God, then...".

This is the same challenge that we are often tempted with. "If you really are a Christian...." Our self-doubts also conspire to contest our heavenly identity. "If God really loved you . . . if you really belonged . . . if you really were on the right path . . . "

As it was in the beginning, so now. There are still reptile forces in and around us that distort God's declaration of what is. We suffer from self-perceived credibility gaps as we picture a great divide between God's word and our assessment of how it plays out in our lives.

We go back and forth from high identities to low ones; from assurance to confusion. "You are saints?.....you are a royal priesthood?....knock and the door will be opened?....surely He is with us always...?" And what is at stake in all this is whether we remain in a state of truth or confusion concerning who we are in Christ.

Jesus was steadfast, in the face of opposition, in defending His identity against those who would have prescribed a much more diminished status for Him. Let us also be steadfast in believing our God-given identity and not settle for a lesser version of who we are in Christ.

29

We do not know how to pray as we ought.

Romans 8:26 (NSRV)

How can we be good students in the school of the Spirit, where the personality of prayer is formed? How does one learn how to "pray as we ought to?" Perhaps the first step is to simply admit that we need help. As Richard Rohr writes, "what often blocks spiritual teaching is the assumption that we already know. We have to always pray for the grace of a beginner's mind." Below, are some simple suggestions for anyone who is ready to call themselves a beginner, gleaned from the experience of people who have learned how to be taught by God.

Before we actually begin praying, St. Ignatius recommends that we first take a moment to remind ourselves of what we are truly seeking. Why are we doing this? What do we hope prayer will lead us to? What is our heart's desire and the hope that we carry into our prayer?

If we want to be taught by the Spirit, David reminds us that we will need to cultivate stillness of soul. The Lord Himself instructed David in this when He told him to "be still and know that I am God" (Ps. 46:10). This quality of soul is most consistent with the nature of God. As the German mystic Meister Eckhart once observed, "nothing in all creation is so like God as stillness."

Remain still in God's presence, letting all things that take place within you simply come under the gaze of your loving Father, without any need to make adjustments for who you are. Whatever you feel, whatever you think, whatever happens, just keep acknowledging the Presence of the Lord in whom you live, move and have your being. In all that you do, simply follow Jesus' instructions to "watch and pray," being observant of the many movements of spirit within you.

The subtle changes in spirit that take place as the minutes unfold are important to observe in prayer. Contemplative prayer involves a process of being transformed from that which does not recognize God to that which does discern God's subtle movement and action in life. Just as an athlete or a musician must first warm up before they feel at one with their idiom, so should we expect transformation in prayer to include a preliminary period of warming up before we can sense God's action within us.

Ultimately, it is only the Holy Spirit who can teach us what it truly means to pray (Rom. 8:27). It is for this reason that the most mature prayer is one that simply allows itself to be guided by the Spirit, without any presumptions of its own achievements or initiatives. As St. John of the Cross taught us, "pure contemplation lies in receiving."

A growing trust with the process of letting go in prayer will allow us to be guided more and more directly by the Holy Spirit as we learn to discern His presence within us. We needn't be too concerned with the results of prayer if we have faith that God, who delights in our obedience, is always directing us in learning how "to pray as we ought." All that is required is an ongoing willingness to be taught."

30

Be careful, or your hearts will be weighed down with dissipation.
Luke 21:34

dis-si-pate: vt. (from the Latin 'dis-supare' meaning to 'throw away') 1. to scatter 2. to make disappear 3. to waste or squander

Jesus gave this warning to His disciples as a way of bracing them against the confusion of the end times. The disciples were secure while in the presence and proximity of Jesus but He warned them, knowing that He would soon depart, to be careful not to let the fine wine of the Spirit become diluted—watered down by the anxieties and distractions of life. It is advice intended for us all—that we not let the many concerns of the day spread our lives out so thin that the concentration of the Spirit would seem to disappear from our souls.

Like sun rays shining through a magnifying glass, the spiritual life needs to be kept in sharp focus if it is to remain intense. With the glass held at an optimum distance the rays concentrate into a burning light. This optimum distance is a very precise one and, as it applies to our souls, is one that we each have to discover and maintain for ourselves. Moving a magnifying glass back or forward, even slightly, will dissipate the rays and weaken their intensity.

Be careful Jesus tells us. It is easy to lose the intensity of your spiritual life. Keep focused. Be aware of the daily state of your spiritual passion and watch for signs of it being squandered.

Jesus goes on to offer an ounce of prevention to help us keep our spiritual focus. "Be always on the watch," He says, "and pray."

Watch— be attentive to the subtle changes that take place in your spirit every day. And pray—take the time to ensure that God's rays remain at optimum focus in you.

31

Blessed are those who hunger and thirst for righteousness for they will be filled.

Matthew 5:6

Hunger and thirst—words that can easily reach a point of desperation. If these words are not satisfied we soon die. For Jesus to apply them to our longing for righteousness implies a level of need that I, for one, have not often experienced. I certainly agree that righteousness is something we should aspire to, and I enjoy those moments whenever I get to taste it in my own life. But something seems to be missing that would cause me to have such an intense desire for it as Jesus expects. What is it that I don't get?

It is obvious that righteousness is something Jesus wants me to pursue more intentionally in my life—with a promise of blessing. According to Jesus, something needs to be filled in my life by what this word represents.

I know from experience a little something of the satisfaction of having behaved, or spoken at times from a place of righteousness. How do I know? Because it feels so right. I sense in those moments that I am exactly what I am supposed to be. And that it is good in God's eyes.

I also sense that righteousness is something that is particular to who I am—that there is some unique expression of righteousness that only I can fulfill. It gets worked out through the subtleties of my personality.

It comes out in the tone of my voice, or in the particular way I look and respond to people. These are life expressions that each of us, original as we are, get to be. In other words, we each have our very own niche of righteousness in the kingdom.

Lest we get too carried away with the idea of our own righteousness, we also read in the Bible that righteousness is not something that we can create ourselves. Our best attempts at it are like rags compared to the real thing that can only come from God. The righteousness that Jesus says will fill us is, in fact, the very spirit of Christ, reflected in the uniqueness of our personality, and in the actions of our life.

Christ's life within us is the free gift of righteousness. There is no credit to be had, no self-congratulation and no such thing as self-righteousness. According to this beatitude, our participation is simply to grow in desire for this gift—to hunger and thirst for the righteousness that God is happy to fill us with. Praise Him for the beauty of His actions within us.

> ... the just man justices;
> Keeps grace: that keeps all his goings graces;
> Acts in God's eye what in God's eye he is -
> Christ. For Christ plays in ten thousand places,
> Lovely in limbs, and lovely in eyes not his
> To the Father, through the features of men's faces.
> —Gerard Manley Hopkins

32

The LORD came and stood there, calling as at the other times, "Samuel! Samuel!" Then Samuel said, "Speak, for your servant is listening."

1 Samuel 3:10

There are many times in life when we are desperate to hear a word from God. What should I do? Where should I go? Who am I? Who are you? Our desire to hear from God often comes from the pressing needs we have for which clear Divine direction would be the most direct remedy. But, in the story of Samuel, we see another disposition towards hearing God's voice—where the need that is being responded to is not ours, but God's.

How often do we feel God tugging at our hearts with an invitation to approach Him? It might not come in the form of a complete sentence but it's easy to know what God is communicating when we sense the gentle breeze of desire for spiritual intimacy pass through our hearts. Perhaps, like Samuel, we need to cultivate the simple response of being attentive to God whenever we feel our hearts being called. Here I am Lord. I heard you call. Speak, for your servant is listening. What would You like from me? For Samuel, listening to God had much more to do with what God might need from him than what he might need from God.

Can we hear the voice of the One who loves us, beckoning our names? We have opportunity, every time we sense God calling us, to respond with the simple act of showing up—to harken as quickly as we can and be attentive.

"Here I am Lord." This was Samuel's posture for listening attentively to God. And in 1Sam. 3:19 it is written, "The Lord was with Samuel as he grew up, and he (Samuel) let none of His words fall to the ground."

That's what it means to be attentive.

33

There remains then, a Sabbath-rest for the people of God; for anyone who enters God's rest also rests from his own work, just as God did from his. Let us, therefore, make every effort to enter that rest.

Hebrews 4:9-10

Isn't there something odd about an exhortation that calls us to "make every effort to enter God's rest?" What is the nature of a rest that requires such effort to enter? It is apparent from the strong wording of this passage that, whatever effort it takes, we are called to seriously consider the concept of a Sabbath-rest as a goal of our spiritual direction, and to cultivate a lifestyle that will allow us to remain in it.

If nothing else, this exhortation is a sober word for anyone who does endeavour to enter God's rest to not underestimate the effort it will take. There are obstacles ahead. And, from what is being said here, it seems that it is our active "work" that is most in the way of our spiritual "rest."

To rest in God simply means to love Him in the full security of faith— to love being with Him more than anything else. If we hold our souls in His presence, not allowing ourselves to be lured away by any other desire or fear of the heart, we will surely have entered the Sabbath-rest that has been prescribed for the people of God. Let us hope, in anticipation of the finished work of the Spirit, that this becomes our increasing experience.

> *It is necessary before all things to obtain tranquility; it is the mother of contentment. The opportunities of practicing it are daily.*
>
> —St. Frances de Sales

34

When anyone hears the message about the kingdom and does not understand it, the evil one comes and snatches away what was sown in his heart. This is the seed sown along the path. The one who received the seed that fell on rocky places is the man who hears the word and at once receives it with joy. But since he has no root, he lasts only a short time. When trouble or persecution comes because of the word, he quickly falls away. The one who received the seed that fell among the thorns is the man who hears the word, but the worries of this life and the deceitfulness of wealth choke it, making it unfruitful. But the one who received the seed that fell on good soil is the man who hears the word and understands it. He produces a crop, yielding a hundred, sixty or thirty times what was sown.

Matthew 13:19-23

If God is continually sowing the seed of His word in my life how much of that seed gets snatched away by the evil one before I'm even aware of it landing on me? How much of it moves my heart for a moment but, as troubles or pleasures distract me, ends up ultimately dying? What percentage of God's word actually takes root and becomes fruitful in me? In short, what type of ground am I?

I am increasingly aware of the changing consistency of the "ground" of my soul throughout the day. At times I find I am quite receptive to God and to other people. At other times I feel closed off, more superficial, less porous. The seed no longer penetrates deeply.

The depth of our ground is certainly one of the things Jesus is drawing our attention to in this parable. The rocky places have no topsoil. There is nowhere for the seed to take root in order to bear fruit. The good ground however is able to receive the seed deeply—to nurture it, to provide it with nutrients, and to remain uncluttered enough for a plant to eventually push through.

A spiritually-minded person spends time preparing the ground of their heart, keeping it loose and receptive through prayer, adding nutrients through study and meditation in order to create the optimum conditions for God's seed to grow. They work to keep the weeds of anxiety and self-pampering at bay so that their ground can be used for more noble purposes. They learn how to nurse the seed to ensure it will germinate after it has touched their hearts. Perhaps they keep a journal so that they can later return and deepen the knowledge or experience that this seed has represented. Or perhaps they introduce new disciplines into their lives, the result of some insight God has shown them about their spiritual growth.

Learning to maintain good ground is one of the most essential conditions for spiritual growth. It is according to the state of your soul that you both receive life as well as beget life. Our "ground" is the place *in* which we are created, as well as the place *from* which we create.

Jesus wants us to consider the ever-changing ground of our souls. If our souls are kept in good condition we will receive God deeply into our lives and bear rich fruit beyond ourselves, into the lives of others. All we do will come from a good place.

> *By their fruit you will recognize them. Do people pick grapes from thorn bushes, or figs from thistles? Likewise every good tree bears good fruit."*
>
> Matthew 7:16-18

35

Let it be unto me, according to Your will.

Luke 1:38

Mary said yes. Certainly God could have bypassed her. He didn't need anybody's consent in order to become a man but could just as easily have come to earth, ex nihilo. But God chose instead to enlist a young girl's "yes."

It is part of the mystery of God's condescension that He sees our yes as a prerequisite before entering more deeply into our lives. Many times in the Bible the Lord's servants are told what He is about to do beforehand. It might seem as though they have no real choice but to accept the will of God. But God particularly chooses to reveal Himself to those whom He knows are already, like Mary, pre-disposed to do His will.

In many ways Mary represents the church as well as the individual Christian life. Following her immortal words, "let it be unto me, according to Your will," the seed that would soon become the fully-formed Jesus entered into her womb. For the next nine months, as Jesus grew within her, Mary's body was transformed. It literally took the shape of God within her as her body stretched to accommodate her growing fetus.

After Jesus was born, Mary's life continued to be shaped by the form her Son's life took. Her yes, though seemingly challenged at times as she observed Jesus' ministry, nevertheless continued to be her disposition as she followed her Son even to the incomprehensible event of the cross. We don't hear much about Mary after the resurrection but we sense, in the few passages we have, that she continued in deep resignation and faith to the will of God in all the circumstances of her life.

As we consider the "seed of Jesus," growing within us in the direction of becoming fully formed, let us consider how our continued yes to God makes room for this seed to expand. Let us see Mary's word not as a one-time statement, but as a daily disposition from which we welcome, with faithful abandon, all the God-ordained circumstances of our lives. This unreserved "yes" is the condition God looks for as He prepares people to do His will.

God looks for the places in us that are trying to say yes.

—Richard Rohr

36

Light has come into the world . . . whoever lives by the truth comes into the light.

John 3:19-21

We live in the shadows. We assume much more concealment than is the case. In John 3 we are encouraged to come out from the darkness where too much mischief, deceit and self-distorting illusions take place, and to step into the Light. The true light of Christ shines on every person born. Let's consider some of the implications of this existential fact of life.

There is nothing that takes place within you that is not in plain, continuous sight of the Lord. There is no thought, concern, hope, fear, truth or lie in you that the Lord is not, at this very moment, aware of. And yet how much of our time is spent in the illusion that our lives are somehow private, hidden from God and from others? Why do we prefer to believe that we are in the shadows rather than in the light?

God's gaze rests on us at all times and therein lies our healing. It is the fundamental truth that sets us free. "Wake up you sleepers!" Paul says (Eph. 5:14). We can understand why the Scriptures want to shake us up from out of our slumber.

To remain awake to the fact that the Lord is intimate with all things that take place within us is nothing other than the contemplative life. It is a freedom that comes from the acceptance that there is nowhere to hide from God. He sees all. We are invited to step into this light of truth—to welcome the Lord in relationship to everything He sees happening in us. We have no reason to fear the light and no reason to prefer the darkness. And that is good news.

He reveals the deep things of darkness and brings deep shadows into the light.

Job 12:22

37

The kingdom of heaven is like yeast that a woman took and mixed into a large amount of flour until it worked all through the dough.

Matthew 13:33

Through the mystery of the Incarnation, God, who created all that is, becomes a part of His creation. Eternity enters the dough of life and begins the work of transforming all things into its own likeness. From a source of life no larger than the size of a baby emanates a Truth so secure and so pervasive that all of life will eventually conform to its correction. According to Jesus' parable, this "yeast" of God will continue to rise throughout creation—until Christ is 'all in all.' This is pretty good news for otherwise flat bread.

You can pull at bread dough all you want from the outside and you will never be able to do more than prop it up a little. But a little bit of yeast mixed into the center of the dough starts working pretty impressively from the inside out. It inflates the dough like a tire and eventually causes it to rise up to a full loaf. We too, like bread, are being raised from the inside out by a divine motion that is leading all of creation upwards towards eternal life.

Like leaven deep in the hearts of men and women, the Holy Spirit is in the process of expanding outwards. As Paul recognized even in the first century, "all over the world this gospel is bearing fruit and growing, just as it has been doing among you since the day you heard it and understood God's grace in all its truth." (Col. 1:6)

We are part of an increasing yield that has been accumulating throughout history since the day Christ was born. In this most subversive way God is reclaiming His creation.

38

Whether you turn to the right or to the left, your ears will hear a voice behind you, saying, "This is the way; walk in it."

Isaiah 30:21

Listen and you will hear. Could it really be that simple? God, directly influencing our way, whether we turn to the right or to the left? It reminds me of the words to an old hymn, "for those who live a life of prayer God is present everywhere." In this passage we find encouragement that, no matter which way we go, we can always hope to hear the Lord's assurances in our prayers: "This is the way, walk in it."

How often do we carry in our minds the image of a fork in the road? We assume that one way is necessarily God's will and that the other will lead us away from His Presence. Though it is always necessary to ask for clarity in making choices it is not appropriate for us to overly fear being out of God's will if we are people of prayer. If we are constantly open to being redirected, His voice is always behind us saying, "This is the way, walk in it."

Jesus knew the assurance of the Father's constant presence when He said in John 8, "the one who sent me is with me; He has not left me alone, for I always do what pleases Him."

This is the same assurance the Lord offered His disciples when He said: "Surely I am with you always, to the very end of the age." Whether you turn to the right or to the left, I am with you always; whether you are in temptation or not, I am always with you always; whether you believe it or not, I am with you always.

You are not lost. This is the way, walk in it. May we be people who listen continually for that blessed assurance.

> *Acknowledge the Lord in all your ways and He will direct your paths.*
>
> Proverbs 3:6

39

Come to me, all you who are weary and burdened.

Matthew 11:28

"Whenever you're feeling tired with life, *come to me.* Yes, I really mean it. Any time you feel burdened or weary, *come to me.* If you're feeling withered—if your soul feels like thorns and thistles—just *come to me*. I will give you rest and restoration."

Jesus invites us to be wise in diagnosing our condition and to not delay coming to Him as needed. He offers Himself as the prescription for what ails the soul. If you're like me you often suffer the effects of life for much longer than you have to because you either don't come to Jesus soon enough, or you're not aware enough of the changing conditions of your soul. Jesus wants us to pay attention to what is happening in our hearts, to follow Prov. 4:23's advice to "guard your heart, for it is the wellspring of life."

In King James English we are called to "walk circumspectly," (Eph. 5:15) i.e., "to walk with eyes inward." A lot happens within us in the course of a day and wisdom calls us to be attentive to these changes since our state of soul determines so much of the direction of our life. The changing conditions in our heart are opportunities for us to hear God's invitation. "Move forward, pause, withdraw, come to me for restoration or new directions." It is important that we learn the skill of walking circumspectly.

The Jesuits have a practice called the Awareness Examen in which, every evening, they pause to examine the effects the day has had on their hearts in light of God's calling. I have adapted the Awareness Examen from a few sources (especially John Veltri S.J.) for our purposes and have copied it below. I would encourage you to adopt this simple prayer as a means of growing in attentiveness to your day.

AWARENESS EXAMEN

This short prayer exercise is to help increase your sensitivity to the Spirit working in your life and to provide you with the awareness needed to co-operate and respond to God's presence. If you use this daily you should find it helpful in noticing spiritual movements and choosing to respond wisely to them. The Awareness Examen is meant as a time of reflection, usually at the end of the day, and can be done in 30 seconds or 30 minutes. It involves five stages:

1. Thanksgiving.

Begin by looking over the day and asking to see where you need to be thankful. Do not choose what you think you should be thankful for, but rather look over the day to see what emerges, what you notice, even slightly. Allow gratitude to take hold of you and express this to the Holy Spirit who at this moment beholds you.

2. Ask For Light

This is a prayer for enlightenment from God. We dispose ourselves for the awareness that we hope will come more directly from God. We have a hard time believing that our own thoughts can actually be from the Spirit but Jesus tells us in Matt 10:20, "it will not be you speaking, but the Spirit of your Father speaking through you." Likewise Paul tells us in Rom. 8 that "we do not know what we ought to pray for, but the Spirit himself intercedes for us with groans that words cannot express." Therefore ask the Spirit to show you what God wants you to pray.

3. Finding God In All Things

Again look over the events of the day. This time ask the Spirit to show you where God's presence has been in your life, either in you or in others, and in the events of your day:

-What events in your day have had an impact upon you?

-Where are the signs of the Spirit, i.e. of light?

-Where are the signs of discouragement of spirit, i.e. of darkness?

-What interior events were significant for you? Notice what stands out even slightly, such as joy, pain, turmoil, increase of love, anger, harmony, anxiety, freedom, isolation, a sense of the presence or absence of God.

-Where do you sense you were being drawn by God's Spirit?

-How did you respond to these events or experiences?

4. Respond To God In Dialogue

Is there any one area you are being nudged to focus your attention on, to pray more seriously over, to take action on? This is where your energy needs focus instead of on the many other things you think are important. Discuss this with Jesus.

Express what needs to be expressed:

... praise ... sorrow ... gratitude ... desire for change ... intercession ...

5. Help And Guidance For Tomorrow

Ask God for your needs for tomorrow. For example, you may need to pray to overcome something ... to be more sensitive to God's activity in your environment ... to celebrate in some way ... to let go ... to be open to conversion in some area ... to make some decisions to act against some destructive forces in your life...to desire a particular grace from God...to desire to desire.

40

No good tree bears bad fruit, nor does a bad tree bear good fruit.
Each tree is recognized by its own fruit.

Luke 6 :43-44

Anyone who regularly practices the Awareness Examen will become much more attentive to what happens within them each day. As we discover the many shades of experience that take place in the course of a day we come to recognize both the good and bad spirits that influence the choices we make. It's important to be able to distinguish between these spirits. In 1 John 4 :1 we are cautioned to "not believe every spirit, but test the spirits to see whether they are from God'" Jesus shows us, in the Scripture above, one way to do this—by examining the fruit a spirit bears within you.

What are you experiencing in your spirit and what has led you there? Is the spirit that has led you to this state of soul truly from God? Or is it a spirit you shouldn't be heeding?

St. Ignatius taught his disciples to distinguish between spirits that produce consolations in the soul and those that produce desolations of the soul. If we picture our inner life as a weather system it might give us an idea of the varied states of light and darkness our souls pass through each day. The word consolation, from the Latin, literally means "with the sun." Desolation, in contrast, means "without the sun." These are important distinctions to note as they each bear quite a different fruit in our spirits.

In his *Spiritual Exercises*, Ignatius identifies the spirit of consolation as causing "an increase of faith, hope, and love, and all interior joy that invites and attracts to what is heavenly by filling it with peace and quiet in its Creator and Lord."

Desolations he defines as:

> darkness of soul, turmoil of spirit, inclination to what is low and earthly, restlessness rising from many disturbances which lead to want of faith, want of hope, want of love. The soul is wholly slothful, tepid, sad and separated, as it were, from its Creator and Lord.

In his diagnosis of the effects of desolation Ignatius adds,

> it is characteristic of the evil spirit to afflict with sadness, to harass with anxiety and to raise obstacles based on false reasoning.

Sound familiar? You will know a spirit by its fruit. A bad spirit produces a souring of the soul. Awareness that this is happening should be the first indicator that the voice you are following is not from God. It is time to let go of whatever your mind, heart or actions have been pursuing and to wait on God for redirection.

The church has handed down to us important wisdom with regards to living the spiritual life. As we learn to pay more attention to our souls we will be able to more wisely choose which voices to follow.

> *My sheep follow me because they know my voice. But they will never follow a stranger; in fact, they will run away from him because they do not recognize a stranger's voice.*
>
> John 10:4-5

41

> *Now the Lord is the Spirit, and where the Spirit of the Lord is, there is freedom.*
>
> 2 Corinthians 3:17

MEDITATIONS FOR SPIRITUAL DIRECTION

In Phil. 2:12 Paul introduced us to the phrase "working out your salvation." It implies that freedom is on its way, but has not exactly arrived yet. There are things that still bind each of us and curtail our experience of freedom in the Lord.

In the slow process of spiritual rebirth we can often feel like a chick being hatched. Even though we know we are free, and faith tells us that we will soon fly, we still seem to be covered with sticky embryonic fluid as we find ourselves pushing outwards against the eggshell of the old person we were. We live in two worlds at the same time. The eggshell is broken open but we're still attached to the familiar comforts of the egg. What do we cling to rather than freedom?

There is an important connection that exists between enjoyment and relinquishment of life. Freedom teaches us to do both—to embrace life, while at the same time learning to detach ourselves from it. Without detachment we are too easily tempted with regret, ambition, anxiety, covetousness and fear to truly enjoy spiritual freedom.

What are you trying to gain in life? What do you fear losing? And how important are such questions to you? The lack of freedom we feel might be a God-ordained occasion to examine how inordinately attached we are to life.

Great faith produces great abandonment—the necessary condition for great freedom.

42

Come, let's go over to the outpost, ...perhaps the LORD will act in our behalf.

1 Samuel 14:6

Do you think the Lord might be calling you to walk in a certain direction but aren't sure? Do you feel that you're sitting on a fence? Are you stalled because you're waiting for some direct word from God before acting? Perhaps you might consider Jonathan's tack of taking a few steps in the direction God might be calling you, just to see what happens.

The Scripture above comes from a fascinating story about Jonathan, the son of King Saul, and his armour-bearer. I think it provides us with a model of faith in action that encourages us to err on the side of curiosity. "I wonder what God would do if I took steps in this or that direction?"

The Israelites, in this story, have been pinned by the Philistine army and are unable to get through a pass in the mountain. Without telling his father, Jonathan suggests to his armour-bearer that they walk over to the Philistine outpost, just to see what the Lord might do with an ounce of bold faith. As Jonathan assures his armour-bearer, "Nothing can hinder the LORD from saving, whether by many or by few."

Jonathan has a simple plan. They will let themselves be seen by the Philistines, who are up on the cliffs. If the Philistines call for them to wait below, they will stay there. But if they tell them to climb up to meet them, they will take this as a sign that the Lord has delivered the Philistines into their hands. I'm not sure where you get theology like this but it's uncanny how effective it often seems to be! In this case the Philistines do invite the men of faith to come up to their camp. And, with the fortuitous help of an earthquake, as well as general panic among the Philistine garrison, Jonathan and his armour-bearer are able to overcome 20 enemy soldiers.

The lesson I learn from such a story is that God welcomes our initiatives. Jesus welcomed Peter's initiative to walk on the water and He welcomes any gumption that is based on our faith and confidence in God. As it was for the disciples, we too have to make decisions at times simply on the basis that "it seems right unto the Holy Spirit."

Is God calling you to act in a certain direction? Does it seem right unto the Holy Spirit? Then why not try taking a few steps in that direction. It's always easier to direct a rolling stone than to try to get a stone rolling.

Let us not allow fear to prevent us from acting. But let's also make sure that we keep attentive to God and how He might further direct us once we've started the ball rolling.

> We must follow our own path and not worry about the puddles into which we fall. The journey itself repairs the accidents into which it has led us. Tidy and timid travellers are never good travellers.
>
> —Abbé de Tourville

43

Praise be to the LORD ,
who has not let us be torn by their teeth.
We have escaped like a bird
out of the fowler's snare;
the snare has been broken,
and we have escaped.

Psalm 124:6-7

Let us consider another side of gratitude—not just for the things we have and the circumstances we enjoy in our lives, but also for the circumstances that never came to be because the Lord's hand was on us. Praise be to the LORD, who has not let us be torn by their teeth.

Consider your life history in terms of forces that might've destroyed, harmed or led you astray if the Lord had not protected you. What circumstances—some of your own making, some created by others—has God's grace helped you escape? What snares has He broken that now no longer entangle you as they once did? Is it time to shout praise and thank the Lord for saving us from what might've otherwise weakened or destroyed us?

The Israelites were careful to never forget the Exodus. The wild party that Miriam led on the safe side of the Red Sea became a model for their celebrations from that time on. The Lord saved them from being torn by the teeth of the Pharaoh's army, and a genuine sense of appreciation for this deliverance was cause for praise and for life-commitment to the God-Who-Saves.

We should similarly consider our life history in terms of God's continuous salvation—remembering times when, given our own inclination, we would likely have strayed; times when we were too weak to care, even for ourselves; times when our own addictions and ambitions caused us to wander aimlessly. The Lord has graciously repaired the messes we've made and still saves us often from the fruit of our own inclinations.

We have escaped the fowler's snare and the Lord is to be praised. He has directed us away from harm and towards safety. He has created circumstances in life that secure and protect us—even from ourselves.

Thank God that things have not turned out as they might have. If the Lord had not been on our side—let Israel say—if the Lord had not been on our side.

Let's take time this week to remember our personal salvation history and may gratitude inspire our response to God's continual care for us.

One of them, when he saw he was healed, came back, praising God in a loud voice. He threw himself at Jesus' feet and thanked him...Jesus asked, "Were not all ten cleansed? Where are the other nine?

Luke 17:15-17

44

Naked came I from my mother's womb, and naked I will depart.

Job 1:21

Picture a football. I think this is something of the shape Job is seeing as he understands the simple truth of life's irony. A football starts as a small point, then bulges in the middle, only to return once again to a very small point.

Our lives have much the same shape. We enter this world in a state of helplessness. We have nothing in our hands, and there is very little we can do about it. As the years pass however, we do accumulate much—possessions, skills, opinions, relationships, an understanding of how things work and a knack for optimizing our lives. But then comes the moment of death when, once again, we find ourselves in a state of incapability. None of the things we have accumulated for life are of any real use to us now. Once again we have nothing in our hands, and there is very little we can do about it.

Every Ash Wednesday, we are reminded that "from ashes we came and to ashes we will go." It's important for us to keep this in mind as we set up our overnight tents here. The book of Job offers another sobering insight, comparing the passage of life to:

> a well-watered plant in the sunshine, spreading its shoots over the garden; it entwines its roots around a pile of rocks and looks for a place among the stones. But when it is torn from its spot, that place disowns it and says, "I never saw you." Surely its life withers away, and from the soil other plants grow. (Job 8:16-19)

Life, as Job understood it, is not a very loyal companion. We are well advised to embrace it without falling into the trap of becoming overly rooted in this place.

The wisdom of contemplative life reminds us that the only permanent feature life has to offer is the Presence of God which graces its folds. The practice of prayer helps us avoid the illusions of permanence and the propensity for accumulation that our minds are so prone to. It helps us recall, as the truest truth, that we are ultimately naked before God.

Naked came I from my mother's womb, and naked I will depart. The contemplative seeks to live this truth today—in simplicity and in poverty of spirit. To build on a foundation other than the one whose architect and builder is God is what the Bible calls foolishness.

What he trusts in is fragile,
what he relies on is a spider's web.
He leans on his web, but it gives way;
he clings to it, but it does not hold.

Job 8:14-15

45

Above all else guard your heart for it is the wellspring of life.
Proverbs 4:23

Where are you situated within yourself? What aspect of yourself do you most identify with? Perhaps a pianist would say his hands. An artist might say her eyes. Many people might say their mouths are the place they feel most identified with. Take a moment before reading on to examine this in yourself. Where are you? Where do you operate from most of the time?

I would imagine (an ironic clue in itself) that most of us identify with our minds more than any other aspect of our being. Our minds lay claim to a significant portion of our personhood. We think, and therefore assume that we are what we think. This Cartesian assumption however can also prove problematic. Many of us know, or have known, what it is like to be victims of our own minds.

The Bible is clear however that we are not our minds. According to Scripture, it is the heart that is the center of who we are. The Hebrew word *labe* (translated "heart") is understood as the seat of our feelings, will and intellect—the place we come *from*, the wellspring of life. That is why the contemplative desires to dwell as much as possible in his or her heart.

The Desert Fathers taught their disciples how to pray with their minds in their hearts. They recognized this as a deepening degree of prayer. As their hearts were warmed by concentration on God their thoughts melted, being transformed more into feelings for God. As Bishop Theophan the Recluse wrote, "whoever has passed through action and thought to true feeling will pray without words, for God is God of the heart."

To find one's heart requires much more simplicity than your mind is usually comfortable with. One has to learn to descend deeper, below the choppy surface waves of who we are. As Simon Tugwell writes,

> What is important is that our prayer should reach down to the core of our being, the point of unity with our identity. This is something deeper than and underlying all our intellectual and emotional activity. It is from there, if anywhere, that our thoughts and feelings can be 'taken captive in Christ.'

It takes grace to recover our heart-identity. But once we have found it, the wisdom of Proverbs tells us to be careful to guard it above all things. Learn how to remain there—in the truth of who you are—because, there, you will discover the wellspring of your life.

Teach me your way, O LORD, and I will walk in your truth; give me an undivided heart.

Psalm 86:11

46

I carried you on eagles' wings and brought you to myself.

Exodus 19:4

In order to talk about the experience of prayer we have to use metaphors or similes. It's a hard thing to describe without being oblique, saying "it's like this or that."

Jesus himself seemed challenged as He tried to put the dynamics of spiritual life into words. "To what shall I compare the Kingdom of Heaven? . . . hmmm . . . it's like a mustard seed . . . no, it's like leaven in the dough . . . actually, it's like a farmer sowing seeds . . . but then again, maybe more like a man building a house." Trying to communicate the subtle nature of prayer inspires an endless variety of images.

I remember watching an eagle once flying high overhead. The eagle had gone through a lot of effort, its muscular wings lifting a considerable weight in order to get to such a height. But once it had reached this altitude its task changed significantly. No longer was flying a matter of effort and hard work. Now it was more a matter of simply learning how to ride the air currents. The slightest adjustment of the wings, of the tail, of the head would allow it to optimize the power of the wind moving all around it. Watching the eagle I could almost feel its excitement as it worked to perfect the art of air-surfing. What subtle attentiveness it requires in order to do this well.

You can't see air currents any more than you can see the Spirit of God. But you can feel them both acting on you and can act wisely in response to them. The eagle was practicing its sensitivity to the air moving all around it. In the environment of the unseen there is no other way to chart a course but by learning how to participate with each passing moment. It's jazz—real improvisation. It's taking whatever comes at you and making the most of it.

There's a sudden gust! Quick, adjust the angle of your wings so that it will lift you up higher. Oh oh, there's an air pocket! Don't worry, just let yourself dip. There must be another air stream just below. I thought I was heading over there, towards the mountain. Guess again, there's a draft turning you back towards the river.

At times the conditions around us dictate that we must lean into the wind in order to harness its strength. Other times they teach us that it's best to just turn around and let the breeze carry us.

As we learn to ride such unseen forces, we discover that a little bit of adjustment goes a long way. Too much effort on our part and we tailspin, and lose our grasp of the idiom. Then we're back to flying on our own again until we rediscover the air currents we were working with before. Too little effort on our part and we never really get off the ground. These are the subtleties that prayer teaches us. It gives us a great respect for the forces acting both around and within us. These forces are our teachers. They guide us, often through trial and error, to make the right adjustments in our lives.

47

Cast your bread upon the waters, for after many days you will find it again.

Ecclesiastes 11:1

One thing that prayer teaches us is that we have to keep letting go in order to advance further. You have to loosen the grip on what is in your hand in order to gain the next thing, or simply to gain a freer relationship to what you already have. Sometimes this requires remaining in a place of nothingness—a place between letting go and receiving—in faith that God will return us to ourselves. We learn to wait, sometimes many days, for what the waters may bring in.

Cast your bread upon the waters. The only way to know for sure that what you have is really God-given is to hold it loosely. Your vocation, your possessions, your status, your lot in life—these are given things. And it is faith that this is so that lets us hold on to them loosely. We cast them back

MEDITATIONS FOR SPIRITUAL DIRECTION

upon the waters of life confident that, if they are from God, they will be found over and over again to be ours.

The alternative to this type of faith is to covet our gifts, fight for our possessions, become anxious about our vocation, or manipulative about securing or bettering our lot in life. We can easily be deceived into thinking we have something to protect.

What is the sustenance (i.e. the "bread") that God is calling you to cast upon the waters? Is it a vision that you are now running headlong with? Is it a status or a security that, after all these years, you have finally achieved? Or is it an anxiety that has been driving you to perform or achieve something in order to feel more significant or complete? Try casting these upon the waters of God's life and see if you don't feel a little freer. Let yourself be surprised at what comes back to you. Notice how the thing has been transformed in its return. It will certainly look different than when it was first in your hands.

48

Although he was a son, he learned obedience from what he suffered and, once made perfect, he became the source of eternal salvation for all who obey him.

Hebrews 5:8

I've always found this Scripture quite a challenge to my sense of Christology. What does the writer of Hebrews mean that Jesus learned obedience, which then made Him perfect? What does it imply for us as we too seek to learn obedience?

When we marvel at an artist in performance, or watch athletes competing in the Olympics, it is impressive to see the high goals they have set and have achieved for themselves. It is daunting to think how much they have had to overcome in order to accomplish these goals. Each of these athletes has learned perfection through overcoming imperfection.

Jesus always seemed to recognize the value of resistance. Perfection is most clearly defined in contrast to all that resists it. Meeting the demands of the Law might be commendable, but Jesus knew that it is in surpassing the Law that perfect obedience is most gloriously displayed.

If someone asks you to walk a mile with them, go two. Don't just love those who love you. That is only meeting the Law. But love those who hate you. That's how love is perfected—in the context of all that naturally resists it.

Jesus was committed to perfectly obeying the will of God. Discerning which village to go to next, what teachings to bring, which disciples to choose was all a matter of seeking God's will in His life. But, as resistance grew in and around Him, the Lord's obedience, according to this Scripture, was being refined. Against His own strong natural desire for self-preservation, and in spite of the counsel of those who tried to dissuade Him, Jesus perfected obedience, even unto death.

What does this mean for you and I as we seek to imitate Christ in our lives? We do our best to obey God. And much of it is pretty easy by now—do not steal, do not murder, do not lie. But where do you feel most challenged? In what areas of your life do you find the most resistance to being obedient? Could this be the very arena that God has provided for you through which to perfect your obedience?

As it was for Jesus so for us. It is in overcoming our natural human resistance to God's will that our spiritual obedience is perfected.

Let us be wise to understand the God-given value of the things in us that seem to resist God—things we would otherwise call failures or weaknesses. These may be the very forums in which obedience is being perfected. As athletes for the Lord we will rejoice to see our inabilities turn into abilities as we are made more and more perfect in the Lord.

And you will stand, for the Lord is able to make you stand.

Romans 14:4

49

When he ascended on high, he led captives in his train.

Ephesians 4:8

Evangelism is incarnational. It is the deep penetration of life by those who carry profoundly within themselves the good news of Jesus

Christ. Evangelism is also incarnational in that it takes on the form of whatever it graces—just like Jesus does with us. It is the leaven that works, from the inside, throughout the dough of life,.

Some people practice surface evangelism. They work on the outside of their subjects, hoping to draw them into contact with the gospel, with themselves, or with the church. The expectation is that they will be able to change people from a distance—to do so without having to step into their world.

The incarnational evangelism that Jesus practices is more like a form of spiritual angioplasty surgery. Angioplasty is a surgical procedure whereby an arterial blockage is expanded with a balloon that is placed within the collapsed artery. As the balloon inflates and rises, it opens up the artery, allowing for improved blood flow. Sometimes a stent, an expandable wire mesh tube, is placed over the balloon. When the stent is expanded along with the balloon inside the artery, it holds the wall open, preventing further narrowing of the arteries. Can you see what I'm picturing here in terms of incarnational evangelism?

Some of us are called to minister deeply into the collapsed veins and arteries of this world. Incarnational evangelists are embedded (which means to be 'set firmly in surrounding matter') in the collapsed world around them. Our task is not to manipulate or coerce this world but to have faith that our very presence within it is part of the process whereby God raises captives in his train. Like a stent that rises to open up arteries, this is kingdom growth that works from the inside out.

God has incarnational evangelists embedded in the business world, in the arts world, in communities, housing projects, neighbourhoods and yes, even in churches. These are people who are not just ministering from the outside, but who are deeply woven into the fabric of the world around them. Like Jesus, they take on the flesh of the world rather than side-step it. This is the incarnational method by which God chooses to redeem us. We are called to also represent this same approach to others.

Incarnational evangelism is simply a matter of living out Jesus' greatest commandment:

Love God... The most you can do for God is to be closely related to those around you.

...and love your neighbour... The most you can do for your friends is to be as closely related to God as you can.

But I, when I am lifted up from the earth, will draw all people to myself.

John 12:32

50

Two are better than one, because they have a good return for their work: If one falls down, his friend can help him up.

Ecclesiastes 4:9-10

How does fellowship keep us from losing sight of the goal of our lives? How do we encourage each other in our pursuit of God? How do we help our friends remember what their hearts are really yearning for?

This familiar Scripture from the book of Proverbs applies to much more than marriage. It is wisdom for the road—for those who appreciate the distance ahead. It recognizes that we can't make the journey very effectively on our own. When we fall, there'll be no one there to help us up. When we forget, there'll be no one to remind us where we're going.

Consider all the outside influences in your life that have helped keep you on the path of pursuing God. How many times has God used others— friends, authors, preachers, casual conversations—to remind you of what your heart is seeking? Consider as well the times when the Lord has used you to encourage and inspire others in this. Two are better than one.

The spiritual life is such that we each have God-given blind spots that often cause us to lose our bearings. We need each other's help in order to remember to stay awake to the presence of God in our lives. Left to ourselves our spirituality would easily go dormant.

According to the diagnosis the Bible offers (especially King James) we have a chronic tendency to faint along the way. Jesus, knowing how difficult it is for us to be persistent in seeking God, speaks a parable exhorting us "always to pray, and not to faint" (Luke 18:1, KJV). Paul also recognizes our propensity to forget that we're on a journey. He sees staying awake as crucial to the fruit we bear as he assures us that "we will reap, if we faint not" (Gal. 6:8-10, KJV). But we can't do it alone. We need outside help.

Most of us would falter without constant reminders of what our faith is. We are like the man in James 1:23 who "looks at his face in a mirror and, after looking at himself, goes away and immediately forgets what he looks like." This is the very mirror we provide for each other in community. We remind ourselves of who we are and where we are going in Christ. Two are better than one...they have a good return for their work.

51

Love your enemies and pray for those who persecute you, that you may be sons and daughters of your Father in heaven.
Matthew 5:44-45

It's hard to love a person who has no use for you, even if their disdain is unspoken. There's a lot of basic psychology to overcome for any of us to love someone who thinks poorly of us. Now imagine if their disdain were expressed in a public way. Imagine them openly mocking you, insulting you. How would that challenge you in your resolve to love? Picture them now walking up to you and spitting in your face. Is there anything more demeaning a person could do to you? How is your love holding up? Next, they beat you, whip you, strike you on the head. Consider how much Jesus had to overcome in order to demonstrate this preaching in practice.

Imagine the Lord, standing in front of an impudent and arrogant King Herod, doing all He can to love in spite of Herod's derision. Picture Jesus before the self-important Pilate, silently loving him in spite of the ironic twist of fate that has given the Governor the illusion that he holds Jesus' fate in his hands. Perhaps silence was the only way Jesus could maintain His inner disposition of love. Perhaps any word spoken might've risked distortion by the resentment that, humanly speaking, Jesus must've also experienced. Forgive them Father for they know not what they are doing.

And finally, picture Jesus being placed on the cross, looking up into the eyes of a man standing above Him, hammer raised, ready to drive a nail through His hand, and loving him. This is love that overcomes all obstacles.

He was oppressed and afflicted, yet he did not open his mouth; he was led like a lamb to the slaughter, and as a sheep before her shearers is silent, so he did not open his mouth. (Isa. 53:7)

What strikes us even more than Jesus' physical suffering is the remarkable victory He had over His inner disposition of love. He allowed all this to happen to Him, without emotional retaliation. Love your enemies and pray for those who persecute you. Jesus shows us the Way.

52

What does "he ascended" mean except that he also descended to the lower, earthly regions? He who descended is the very one who ascended higher than all the heavens, in order to fill the whole universe.

Ephesians 4:8-10

On a cosmic level two things are taking place simultaneously in life—the Fall and the Resurrection. The Fall pulls things down, subjecting them, as Paul says, to the laws of decay and death. The Resurrection, in spite of this, raises things upwards, in the direction of renewal and life.

Everywhere we look we can see signs of the Fall, the dis-integration in life, as well as signs of the Resurrection, the integration in life. In all our relationships, in the structures of our society, in world history, even in our own souls, we witness the action of life coming together, as well as that of life falling apart. One causes hope, the other despair.

The word *dia-bolic* means to "throw apart." From Adam's first sense of separation from God to this day we have all suffered the dia-bolic effects of the Fall in our lives.

When we are under the dis-integrating influence of the Fall we feel alone, disjointed, without a centre, divided in mind and spirit. Anyone who lives in community knows the alienating effect this force can have on our relationships.

But Jesus entered into the very depths of this dis-integration. He descended to the lower regions of the earth in order to attach Himself to the Fall—to all that is dying—and then to be raised up, so that all that is attached to Him may be raised up as well. As Christ ascends on high, He leads all that was subject to the law of death and decay upwards towards life. He is the head, in whom all things will once again be integrated.

As Christians, we are called to be active participants in the Resurrection action of Christ in this world. We follow our Lord as He descends into the "lower earthly regions"—to places that suffer from dis-integration. And we bear witness to His Resurrection deep within these places. We work, watch and pray for signs of the promise that "the creation itself will be liberated from its bondage to decay and brought into the glorious freedom of the children of God" (Rom. 8:19-21).

As followers of Christ we are called to position our lives in such a way as to best participate with Jesus as He counters the effects of the Fall all around us. And we celebrate everything that holds together in Christ as a glorious sign of Resurrection hope.

53

This is what the kingdom of God is like. A man scatters seed on the ground. Night and day, whether he sleeps or gets up, the seed sprouts and grows, though he does not know how. All by itself the soil produces grain—first the stalk, then the head, then the full kernel in the head. As soon as the grain is ripe, he puts the sickle to it, because the harvest has come.

Mark 4:26-29

Where, and at what stage is your ministry? Or to use Jesus' metaphor, what is the maturity of the grain in your soil? Perhaps the seed is still at the sprouting stage. You believe that you have a ministry but you don't know what it is yet. Every now and then you feel definite promptings of love and joy that deeply move the desires of your heart. It could just be a wish, a dream, or a direction of how you would love to be applied in life. As you continue to nurture and care for that mysterious seed buried within you, visible stalks eventually appear above ground as you recognize opportunities in life to cultivate the seed further. It might be a person you meet who shares a similar vision, or an opening to volunteer with a group that is doing something in the general direction of your calling. Perhaps you feel led to take initiative in equipping yourself to serve better in this area.

As you continue discerning, not only from the promptings within you but now also from the formation that comes from the outside, your plant soon develops its head. You know with greater confidence who you are in life and you now move with a stronger sense of purpose towards intentional ministry. It's a slow process that can't be hurried any more than you can rush your geraniums into bloom.

And if your ministry should grow to the stage of producing a "full kernel in the head," it will now have its own reproducing seed. God will use your ministry as a way of birthing something similar in another person. It's an amazing process that is always taking place throughout the kingdom of God.

In all these mysteries of spiritual growth one thing is certain. We are all being applied in ministry by virtue of the salt and light that Jesus' increasing Presence represents within us. Believe that kingdom ministry is taking place through you and you will certainly see it happening. We don't look for, nor choose a ministry as though we didn't have one. But, by being more attentive to the plant that God is growing within us, we discover the one we already have .... first the stalk, then the head, then the full kernel in the head.

54

Be clear-minded and self-controlled so that you can pray.

1 Peter 4:7

Praying doesn't start when you sit down to pray. That's the time you get to go deeper from wherever you are. But this question of the shifting state of "wherever you are" is important to our prayer experience. Our state of soul keeps fluctuating throughout the days and weeks and we need to be reminded that we have opportunity to steer it always in the general direction of prayer.

For centuries contemplatives have tried to pursue Paul's instructions to "pray unceasingly" (1 Thes. 5:17). This of course can't mean to be in constant dialogue, or monologue, with God every minute of the day.

Unceasing prayer is to be understood as more of a grace of spirit that pervades the day. It's an ongoing openness and attentiveness to God's action within us that gets cultivated throughout our lives. And according to Peter, in order to be prayerfully attentive we first need to be clear-minded. What does this imply for our day?

If we think of a water well whose surface is perfectly still we might get an idea of what Peter means. When the water surface is still and calm, you can sometimes see all the way to the bottom of the well. But if the water is being constantly stirred up or splashed around it's hard to see anything beyond the surface.

Let's not underestimate the effect a day's agitations can have on our spirit of prayer, nor the opportunity we have to counter this by practicing stillness each day. As prayer becomes more and more central to our lives we will learn to interpret everything in terms of what contributes or detracts from it, and we will make life-style changes accordingly. We will apply self-control to our inner life for the sake of a better relationship to prayer.

If we seek such peace and learn to pursue it in our day, prayer will certainly be the natural expression of minds that are controlled by the tranquility of God.

> *In patience you shall possess your souls. To possess fully our souls is the effect of patience, made more perfect as it is less mixed with disquiet and eagerness.*
>
> —St. Frances de Sales

55

> *Ask and it will be given to you; seek and you will find; knock and the door will be opened to you. For everyone who asks receives; whoever seeks finds; and to they who knock, the door will be opened.*
>
> Luke 11:7-8

Jesus' words in Luke were given in response to the disciples asking Him how they should pray. Jesus here teaches us the disposition we should maintain while awaiting an answer to prayer. We have our role to play in this relationship, and so does God. And we need to learn how to make room for God's part.

If we look at the grammar in this passage we see two sides of the prayer coin: the active and the passive parts. This is the gracious dance of faith that prayer leads us to.

Ask and it will be given to you. Is our disposition towards the things we ask for in prayer that of a person preparing to receive something, or is it more like someone expecting to get something? A "getting" posture is one that counts on prayer to achieve the outcome we desire. We already know what we want and we're hoping that prayer will secure it for us. A "receiving" posture, on the other hand, doesn't presume the shape our petition will take as God hands it back to us in the form of an answered prayer. It takes practice in prayer in order to learn how to receive freely from God, i.e. to allow something to be given to you.

Seek and you will find. We have images of God, of ourselves, and of life that we keep returning to for assurance. There is nothing really to "find" in this type of prayer. To seek means to look for something we don't already have. It's the prerequisite to the authentic experience of finding—more like a child discovering something brand new, something they would've never imagined existed. It takes faith in prayer to be open to finding things we weren't necessarily expecting.

Knock and the door will be opened to you. Once again the same grammar applies. We can push doors open on our own, sometimes even producing the results we wanted. The satisfaction though is very different from that of knowing that a particular door has been opened for us by God. There is no greater security in spiritual direction than to know that the Lord is inviting you to walk through a door that He Himself has opened. It takes patience in prayer to wait in front of a closed door, giving God the freedom to open it or not.

Trusting God is the essence of prayer, and Jesus assumes that, given what we know of Him, this disposition should be so natural for us as to make the alternative laughable. That's why He ends this teaching with the ridiculous notion of a son who would ask his father for a fish, only to get a snake instead (Luke 11:11-12). The son then asks for an egg, and his father gives him a scorpion. It's ridiculous to think that a father would act this way towards his child. But is this what our fears and anxieties sometimes look like from God's perspective? How does peace of mind, and confidence in His provisions, honour God's care for us?

To wait until our prayers are answered before allowing ourselves to have peace is to miss out on Jesus' great teaching here. Prayers are meant to produce peace in us, long before they are answered.

56

To the faithful you show yourself faithful,
to the blameless you show yourself blameless,
to the pure you show yourself pure,
but to the crooked you show yourself shrewd.

Psalm 18:25-26

According to this psalm, God's image within us, his "imago dei," is reflected upon whatever condition of soul His light finds. As Jesus taught us, "with what measure we meet so it will be met to us" (Mark 4:24). The soul that obscures itself from God sees an obscured God, whereas the soul that openly faces God permits a purer reflection. Like a diamond turning in the light, different facets of God reveal themselves depending on how we relate to Him.

Paul says that, for the sake of ministry, he has learned to become all things to all people (1 Cor 9:22). He adapts himself according to what the person he is ministering to gives him to work with. Perhaps this is another insight into how God mirrors, for the sake of our spiritual growth, whatever is necessary for Him to be with us.

Psalm 18 reminds us that a lot of our experience of God comes from what we project into the relationship. God is changeless, but our perception of Him is always in flux. As our "mirroring" becomes more sanctified, purity allows God to increasingly reveal Himself to us as He is.

The mirror gets polished, the smudges removed, the distortions corrected, and we see the Lord more and more as He truly is. And this very hope—of reflecting more accurately the "imago dei" within us—helps purify our spiritual direction. As John puts it,

What we will be has not yet been made known. But we know that when He appears, we shall be like Him, for we shall see Him as He is. Everyone who has this hope in him purifies himself, just as He is pure. (1 John 3:2-3)

Blessed are the pure in heart, for they will see God.

Matthew 5:8

57

Wisdom is supreme; therefore get wisdom.
Though it cost all you have, get understanding.
Esteem her, and she will exalt you;
embrace her, and she will honor you.
She will set a garland of grace on your head
and present you with a crown of splendor.

Proverbs 4:7-9

Wisdom is the prize of life. It is worth more than silver and gold. Nothing we desire compares with it. As chapter after chapter in the book of Proverbs teaches us, wisdom comes with the knowledge of God. To learn wisdom one needs only to pursue God.

As we seek God—or "call out for insight and cry aloud for understanding" (Prov. 2:3)—wisdom teaches us the fear of the Lord and how to walk more securely in the knowledge of His ways. There is nothing more beneficial to life.

...then you will understand what is right and just
and fair—every good path.
For wisdom will enter your heart,
and knowledge will be pleasant to your soul.
Discretion will protect you,
and understanding will guard you.   (Prov. 2:9-11)

Wisdom is full of truth and grace. Her ways are pleasant, and her paths bring peace. We recognize it as "from above"—as originating from the very character of God.

Wisdom is a quality of life, and those who lay hold of her are blessed. They walk in the light of understanding and nothing makes them stumble (Prov. 4:12). Wisdom teaches us how to be careful in life, when to embrace it and when to show restraint.

I, wisdom, dwell together with prudence;
I possess knowledge and discretion.   (Prov. 8:12)

Wisdom is hospitable. It beckons us in from the streets and opens its doors wide to anyone who knocks. "I love those who love me, and those who seek me find me" (Prov. 8:17). We ignore her at our own peril. Whoever fails to find me harms themselves (Prov. 8:36).

Simply said, wisdom is knowing how to interpret life in the knowledge of God's ways. As we place ourselves increasingly under the action and influence of Truth, wisdom guides us to the knowledge of who God is, and of who we are. In turn it blesses our lives and bears good influence in the quality of our ministry . . . therefore get wisdom.

For whoever finds me finds life
and receives favor from the LORD.
If you are wise, your wisdom will reward you

Proverbs 8:35, 9:12

58

He makes me lie down in green pastures,
he leads me beside quiet waters,
he restores my soul.

Psalm 23:2-3

People go to chiropractors when they feel their bones are out of alignment. One disc out of joint sets the whole vertebrae into painful compensation. Luckily, the skilful hand of a chiropractor can tell what is out of line and can physically manipulate it back into place. With everything set in right order there is peace and proper functioning once again in the body.

As I come to prayer, I am often similarly aware that my spirit is out of sorts. I feel internally crippled, as though my soul was in some contorted state. Perhaps it has been battered by my emotions, or is in a spasm over a disturbing thought I have been obsessing about. Sometimes it is fear that causes my soul to close in on itself, tightening its grip and cutting off the circulation of the Spirit within me.

Like chiropractice, prayer is also a time for setting things in their right order. The shrivelled hand is restored to its original shape. That which is lame is made free to walk again. That which was blind can now see and what was deaf can once again hear. Only the Holy Spirit knows what my restored self looks like and, as I trust in God's re-creative power, I am once again set in right order through prayer.

Before a chiropractor can manipulate your bones however you must first learn to relax. If you remain tense you can actually worsen your condition. Similarly with prayer, the Holy Spirit works according to the degree of trust we have. As we rest in God, there are times when we can actually feel the gentle manipulations of the Spirit working deep within our soul as slight adjustments are made, freeing up the movements of our spiritual life.

But, as anyone who goes unfortunately knows, a visit to a chiropractor is not a one-time event. No sooner do we step out of the clinic, refreshed and in proper alignment, do we start walking, bending, sitting according to all the bad habits that brought us there in the first place. It can be a costly and very temporary recovery program. Lucky for us though, as it applies to prayer, we have a great medical plan in heaven that allows us to return to the Great Physician as often as needed for restoration.

May wisdom teach us to not delay before seeing the Doctor at the first symptoms of spiritual contortion.

59

Blessed are those whose strength is in you, who have set their hearts on pilgrimage. As they pass though the valley of Baca, they turn it into springs.

Psalm 84 :5-6

Geese know how to organize in a V formation in order to give them optimum efficiency when flying in a group. An air turbulence is set up by the geese ahead which carries you further than the effort you are expending. Something similar seems to happen when you fly around those who have "set their hearts on pilgrimage," i.e. those who are cultivating the pursuit of God in their lives. You find yourself being carried further than you ever could on your own.

To pursue God is to blaze a trail that gets deeply etched in life. But it is not just for ourselves that this path exists. Our individual journeys give courage and direction to those around us as well. Like a boat that sets its point forward through the water there is a wake that forms, influencing the direction of things behind it.

When I was younger I had a small motor boat and would often go for trips on the St. Lawrence River. Big ships passed through the channel each day and, if I wanted to make better speed coming home, I could easily put myself in the wake of a cargo ship and be carried swiftly alongside it.

A person who has cultivated the discipline of prayer in their lives likewise has a life-turbulence around them that seems to encourage a similar direction in those who are near. Anyone with vitality in their prayer life naturally inspires those who sense similar possibilities for themselves. They remind those around them of what is also the deepest desire of their hearts. Love for God is contagious and it is something that is usually caught more than taught.

Isn't this the way God always seems to work? Not only do we benefit from His Presence, but He ordains that there is a spillover effect whereby dry deserts turn into springs of life. As we are drawn to God, the Lord takes occasion, through us, to draw others as well.

Consider the people, both past and present, who have had this effect on you—those whose intimacy with God has reminded you of your own spiritual potential—and you will know the phenomena that the psalmist is describing here: as they pass through the valley of Baca, they turn it into springs.

60

The kingdom of heaven is like treasure hidden in a field. When a man found it, he hid it again, and then in his joy went and sold all he had and bought that field. Again, the kingdom of heaven is like a merchant looking for fine pearls. When he found one of great value, he went away and sold everything he had and bought it.

Matthew 13:44-46

It's hard to find time to pray. And even when we do, it's often a struggle to keep focused on seeking God rather than pursuing the many other interesting thoughts and tangents that come to mind. The discipline of prayer is certainly a forum where making good spiritual choices is a constant challenge. As one of my mentors, Dr. James Houston, once said, "Prayer is ultimately a battle of the will. The battle makes us choose what, in the end, we really want."

This first parable tells us of man who stumbles upon a treasure and then takes steps to secure what he really wants. Likewise, when the merchant of the second parable finds a pearl of great price, he goes and sells all he has in order to purchase it. In both cases the assumption is that the person does not yet possess the desired item, but has to acquire it through an exchange of goods. He has to sell what he has in order to get what he would prefer having. To think of our prayer life in such consumerist terms can be helpful. Consider these three parallels:

The first would be to compare having read about prayer, and feeling excited about the possibility of acquiring such an experience for ourselves, with catalogue shopping. The items in a catalogue are meant to draw our attention to their selling features and to convince us to purchase them. At some point the catalogue has done as much as it can and it's now up to us to choose whether we want this item for ourselves or not.

A second, more developed relationship to prayer might be compared to window-shopping, or browsing in a store. You can spend a lot of time examining a beautiful jacket that you're considering purchasing. You can look at it from all angles, feel its material, perhaps even try it on for size. And you can come back the next day to do the same thing all over again.

But as much as you admire the jacket, it will never be yours until you've actually bought it. You can't take it out of the store until you've exchange goods for it.

And lastly, a third relationship to prayer might be compared to test-driving an expensive car. If we've had even minimal practice in the discipline of prayer, it's likely that God has allowed us to experience some of the delights of spiritual experience first-hand. Like any salesman who believes in his product, it would be fair for God to assume that, having now sampled the goods, we will quickly empty our wallets to secure this wonderful item for ourselves.

It would be an odd parable wouldn't it, if Jesus had spoken of a man who found a pearl of great value but, though excited and intent on buying it, got distracted on his way to the bank by a piece of granite on the side of the road. And yet wouldn't this be an apt description of the way we often stray from our spiritual goals?

What keeps us on track? In this parable, Jesus tells us that it is joy for our goal that directs us. It's what kept the merchant focused on his intentions—in his joy, he went and sold all he had. Because of the joy we have experienced in His Presence, Jesus expects us to make it a priority to sell all we have in order to procure this precious pearl. It is surely worth more than anything else we could ever desire.

61

Thy will be done on earth as it is in heaven.

Matthew 6:10

This petition is certainly the underlying prayer of the contemplative life. Thy will be done....and let it begin with me. When everyone on earth reflects this prayer we will live as a multitude of perfectly orchestrated expressions of God, in other words, heaven on earth. I suspect there is an inner sense in us that already knows that such a day is not only possible, but the inevitable solution to all that is wrong with life.

As we pursue God through prayer, a spiritual intuition is at work in us that desires, above all things, to find and follow the immediate will of

God. We sense a distortion in our lives that confuses our personalities, our direction, and the effect we have on others. We recognize the dubious nature of the choices we make and how they contribute to the disarray around us. And something in us suspects that the solution to this discrepancy lies in a more perfect obedience to the will of God.

The fact that Jesus put these words in our mouths is proof enough that "what is" is not "what should be." That we pray for God's will to be done on earth is an acknowledgment that we recognize a re-alignment is necessary in order for us to become what heaven truly has in mind.

But Jesus isn't telling us to get to work correcting this problem. That would be an impossible task. As T.S. Eliot put it, "Out of the crooked timber of humanity, no straight thing was ever made." Instead, the Lord offers us a remedy in the form of a prayer that looks to God for both personal and social transformation. These eleven words recognize that such restoration can only come from above.

To be willing to submit to a Way that is higher than ours is what is implied in the petition, "Thy will be done on earth as it is in heaven." And the request that this prayer expresses is what is most required of us in order for it to be fulfilled—the sincere longing that it be so in our own lives.

62

Deep calls to deep
in the roar of your waterfalls;
all your waves and breakers
have swept over me.

Psalm 42:7

Do you remember being at the beach as a child, digging a hole in the sand and then watching it fill up with water? Because the water table is so high you don't have to dig very deep before it comes pouring in. But soon after, mud starts falling in from the edges, fills the hole, and once again you have to dig out new space for the water. When I remember this I can't help but feel there's something very similar happening in my spiritual life. It also helps me understand the relationship between my spiritual disciplines and the infilling of God's spirit.

The contemplative life, in a very basic sense, is a matter of creating holes in anticipation of God filling them. There are lots of ways we can dig holes in our lives: fasting, prayer, silence, humility, tithing, submission, etc. These disciplines create space within us. But as our childhood experience teaches us, it doesn't take very long for the ocean to fill a hole that is dug close to the shore. We know how the contours of our lives, like sand falling in from the edges, soon begin filling up the hole again. That's why it takes ongoing spiritual disciplines to keep space open for God.

As Deep calls to deep we are led to what is most profound within us. To be a spiritual person is to learn to live deeply. The very word *profound* is a composite of the Latin for *pro,* meaning "toward," and *fundere,* which means "bottom." The word that contrasts with this depth of life is the word *superficial,* which means to be "above the face," to remain on the sur-*face* of things. Being shallow is a concept that can easily apply to our spiritual life at times.

But God wants better for us. He calls us to live deeply. And prayer is the prescribed exercise for finding and remaining in the place that is most profound within us. As we discover the depth of wisdom and truth that lies in each of us, Psalm 42 testifies to the experience of God's infilling Spirit rising up, like Living Waters, within us. All your waves and breakers have swept over me. Let us dig deep holes and, in faith, live lives where being "swept over by God" might often be our experience as well

63

Whoever believes in me, as the Scripture has said, streams of living water will flow from within him.

John 7:38

In her wonderful booklet, *The Prayer Life as a Garden,* St. Teresa of Avila speaks of four stages of prayer. These are not necessarily progressive steps, nor are they experiences that everyone who prays will recognize as consistent with theirs. But they are helpful markers of a direction that Jesus promised would well up in all those who enter and pursue God's stream of life.

Teresa calls us to be good gardeners of our lives who, with the help of God, must see that our spiritual plants grow. "We should water them carefully that they will not die, but rather produce blossoms." She describes four ways by which we can water our garden, beginning with the most labourious, and ending with the most effortless.

The first way is compared to simply drawing water in a bucket from a well. This refers to the effort of being disciplined in prayer, returning to it often, and drawing what we can from meditating on thoughts of God. "Working with the understanding then, is like drawing water out of the well." This form prayer she calls meditation.

The second way of prayer is like a water wheel which draws the water up from the well for you. You arrive at the well to find a bucket, already full of water. This, Teresa compares to the prayer of contemplation, which "now touches on things that are divine, which it could never do by any effort of its own." It is a time when grace freely reveals itself to the soul. Our wills have somehow become subject to God's will. We now merely consent to being captured by the love of God. Teresa writes,

> Everything that takes place now in this state brings the very greatest consolation. The labour is so light that prayer, even if persevered in for some time, is never wearisome. The reason is that the understanding is now working very gently and is drawing much more water than it drew out of the well.

In this mode, the soul dares not move nor stir for fear that the blessing it is receiving would then disappear from its hands. Teresa stresses that "it is very important that the soul which reaches this stage realize the great dignity of its position and the great favour that the Lord has bestowed upon it." The soul, through this experience, becomes aware of a love it has for God that is much less self-interested. It now desires to find solitude more often in order to enjoy that good love all the more.

Teresa then describes a third way of prayer which is like finding streams in your garden that only require being directed towards the flowers. The soil is now more thoroughly saturated and there is no necessity to water it as often. The labour of the gardener is simply that of directing the stream that flows constantly into its garden, towards the flowers. In this state of prayer there is less distinction between our work and God's work within us. We assume more readily that the life welling up within us is, in fact, the Holy Spirit. It is contemplation in action. Our will is active, but mostly in consenting to the action of God within us. If the second way of praying was more characteristic of Mary, sitting without stirring at Jesus' feet, this third way Teresa likens to also include the active nature of Martha. "The soul is living both the active and the contemplative life at the same time." It is active in the world and yet understands that "the best part of the soul is somewhere else."

Finally, the fourth way of prayer is when you find that it is raining all around you. The garden is being watered all by itself and there is nothing left for you to do. This is the effortless perfection of receiving our lives completely from the hand of God. The heavenly water "flows to our very depths and spreads within us." In terminology that we can only imagine, Teresa refers to this experience as "the soul entering within itself." This is the Mystical Union with God that so many saints have spoken of.

People who often pray will likely recognize elements of each of Teresa's four stages in their prayer experience. For those who are just being introduced to the fruit of prayer, Teresa's words will hopefully excite your heart and help identify a real passion that exists within you for love and intimacy with God. Either way, it is wonderful to have spiritual ancestors like Teresa who write from an experience that confirms the heart's instinct and desire for union with God. Whoever believes...streams of living water will flow from within. Let us be encouraged to seek growth in the knowledge of God so freely offered, in Jesus' words, to "whoever believes."

64

For in him, we live, move and have our being.

Acts 17:28

I had a strange dream once. I'm not usually inclined to fantasy in my dreams but this one certainly had all the elements of a Twilight Zone episode. The fact that this dream created such a change of perception in my life tells me that it was probably a "Word of God"—the type that doesn't come back empty but accomplishes what the Lord sent it out to do.

In the dream I had somehow ended up in the middle of outer space, suspended on a cube-shaped scaffold. All around me, in every direction as far as could be imagined, there was nothing but infinity. The scaffold was the only thing I had to hold on to. As I was trying to come to terms with my predicament, I suddenly became aware of a large hand materializing out of nowhere. With thumb and finger it began pulling at one of the bars of the scaffold. I somehow knew that this hand belonged to God and I immediately protested, "Why are you doing this?" The hand ignored me and then disappeared, taking with it one of the supporting bars of the cube. My state of affairs was now even more precarious than before. After the initial shock had subsided, having no other choice, I accepted my loss and went back to contemplating my options.

It wasn't long before the hand reappeared and started pulling once again at another bar. Again I went through all the motions of shock and protest, as well as the confusion of why God was doing this. But the hand continued its merciless work of dismantling the structure that was keeping me afloat. This same exercise repeated itself again and again until finally, I was left with one remaining bar—the only thing keeping me from falling into the deep abyss below. And once more, to my horror, the hand reappeared.

I remember pleading with God, explaining how I will fall if He removes this last bar (as though He didn't understand my predicament). But my cries went unheeded as the hand reached out to remove the last remaining bar. I braced myself for whatever would happen next as I felt the bar slowly being pulled out from the tight grip of my hands.

Somehow I still had faith that God would not let me fall, but how? Would He quickly reach underneath to rescue me? Would He offer me His own hand to hold onto? Or would He create another scaffold below me to land on? I waited, bracing myself for whatever might follow. But nothing happened. To my surprise, I didn't fall. I was still floating in open space, in the same place where the scaffold had been. My belief that the structure was what had been keeping me afloat turned out to be an illusion. And all my fears, as well as the emotional investment the scaffold represented to me, were for nothing. Sound familiar?

MEDITATIONS FOR SPIRITUAL DIRECTION

This was a dream that challenged me to take stock of all the other scaffolds in my life that I presumed to be supporting me. It was also a call for me to start exercising more faith in the free-fall of life. It taught me that, as long as I am holding on to my self-made securities, I will never recognize the security of the God who is actually sustaining me.

In Him, we live, move and have our being. The contemplative life invites us to let go of our self-made constructs in order to discover God, the One who actually sustains us.

65

When the woman saw that the fruit of the tree was good for food and pleasing to the eye, and also desirable for gaining wisdom, she took some and ate it. She also gave some to her husband, who was with her, and he ate it.

Genesis 3:6

In his book *The Shattered Lantern,* Ronald Rolheiser offers a unique interpretation of the Adam and Eve story. As we know, in the story of the Fall, the Lord places Adam and Eve in a garden, a rich environment that ideally provides for all their needs. He gives them simple instructions that could be paraphrased as:

"Receive all I have given you, but do not take for yourself that which I have not given you."

Our first parents are showered with the goodness of life, and a promise that this blessing will continue all their days. The one restriction placed on them is that they should not take, or covet this life, as if it were theirs by right or claim. It is an important lesson on the disposition of freedom we are to exercise in relation to the gift of life. We can almost hear God's word blessing them through these instructions:

> As long as you continue to receive and respect reality as a gift, it will continue to give you life and goodness. But as soon as you attempt to actively seize it, or when you take it as something owed to you, life will decrease and there will be shame, loss of harmony, and a loss of proper connection with God.

In the story of the Fall we can see the origins of our distorted attachments to life—our coveting of that which was meant to be gift. Consider the manipulations of life and its outcomes in the subsequent actions of Cain, the builders of Babel, the producers of the golden calf, Abraham and Hagar, and David's reclaiming of the Ark of the Covenant and you see this pattern repeated over and over again. We see as well how quickly God's correctives move in to prevent this approach from becoming the norm. Why is this so important to God?

When a child is caught sneaking off with a cookie from the forbidden jar, it is likely not the cookie that the mother is concerned with. Long after the cookie has been eaten and digested what remains within the child is the knowledge that they have taken something that they shouldn't have. The inner condition that results in the child is very opposite to the delight which would come, to both mother and child, from the cookie being received as a gift.

Perhaps this is the reason God insists that we not lose the only relationship to life appropriate for created beings—that of gift. It is a question of not forfeiting the truth of who we are. As Rolheiser says elsewhere, "receptivity and gratitude lie at the root of purity of heart." It is also at the root of our praise to God as the Giver of life. We owe it to our Creator to delight in the gift of life and creation. And to act as though it were ours for the taking is to rob the Lord of His due.

By the grace of God's restoring Spirit we are being healed of our tendencies in this area. Our minds are being transformed towards that which more fitly recognizes life as gift, and which honours God as Giver. Ronald Rolheiser refers to what is being restored as our *contemplative faculty* and offers this prescription for encouraging spiritual health:

> The first exercise we must do to restore our contemplative faculty is to work at receiving everything—live, health, others around us, love, friendship, food, drink, beauty—as gift. To the extent that we take life for granted we will never see the Giver behind the gift. But once we stop taking life for granted we will soon enough begin to feel it as it really is—granted to us by God.

66

Now the LORD God had formed out of the ground all the beasts
of the field and all the birds of the air. He brought them to the
man to see what he would name them; and whatever the man
called each living creature, that was its name.

Genesis 2:19

This passage reveals how honoured we are in the relationship God chooses to form with us. It shows us how our Father delights and is keenly interested in how we respond to His creation. When we read that the Lord brought the animals to Adam in order "to see what he would name them," it implies a certain amount of uncertainty that we don't usually ascribe to God. He is curious about how we will respond, and He looks to us to put the final label on what He has created. Perhaps this delight is the same as that of a father giving a kitten to his child and waiting to see what she will call it.

To name something, of course, is more than simply giving it a label. It expresses a relationship or an impression we have of something. It is how we respond to the thing before us.

If God leaves the final interpretation of His creation up to us, how does this apply to the various circumstances He brings before our lives? What are the "names" we give to these circumstances? Fearful? Opportunity? Good? Bad? Punishment? Reward? Success? Failure? A test? A blessing? And how does the "name" we give contribute to how we experience them? "Whatever the man called each living creature, that was its name."

The naming of things is one of the noble privileges God has given us, but it can also be a two-edged sword if we're not careful with the names we choose. What we call something will determine the relationship we form with it. Jesus once told His disciples "what is bound on earth is bound in heaven." We need to be careful to not be too hasty in choosing names.

67

The Pharisee stood up and prayed about himself: "God, I
thank you that I am not like other men—robbers, evildoers,
adulterers—or even like this tax collector. I fast twice a week and
give a tenth of all I get." But the tax collector stood at a distance.
He would not even look up to heaven, but beat his breast and
said: "God, have mercy on me, a sinner." I tell you that this man,
rather than the other, went home justified before God

Luke 18:11-14

You can't tell a book by its cover, and sometimes even its content can deceive us. According to this parable, our inner feelings about our status with God are not always the best judge of where we stand. How often, in the paradox of spiritual life, might our sense of distance from God actually indicate our closeness to Him? And how might our feelings of self-satisfaction with our spiritual life actually be an indicator of a tepid spirit?

The Pharisee thought himself to be in a state of consolation. He was enjoying a wonderful sense of well-being with regards to his relationship with God. In his mind all things were as they should be. He stood confidently before the Lord, giving thanks for the abundant blessings of his life.

Acknowledging God's grace is of course the great antidote to the sense of self-accomplishment that so often tempts a blessed life. No danger of that faux-pas for this saint. The Pharisee acknowledged his good fortune, and didn't hesitate to give all the glory back to God. He felt satisfied, highlighting the obvious evidence of his gratitude—his regular disciplines of fasting and tithing. You can just hear the beginning words of the hymn forming on his lips, "It is well, it is well with my soul."

The tax collector, on the other hand, stood at a distance. Not only physically, but also in his sense of relationship to God. Ignatius describes the state of desolation as that of feeling separated from our Creator. The Lord allows such experiences at times in order to purify our love, our faith and our desires. Standing near the real Presence of God has always led saints to a sober awareness of their relative unworthiness.

In Jesus' parable, the Pharisee was the one who was blind to the truth. He presumed God's favour and was immune from correction. Though he felt accomplished in his spiritual life, this sense of well-being was unfortunately an illusion—the fabrication of his own imagination—and not a true consolation from God.

The tax collector, humble and contrite, could not even imagine himself in relationship to heaven. He felt alienated from God. It was all he could do to muster the faith to set foot in His house. "I tell you that this man, rather than the other, went home justified before God."

How important are our own judgments of our spiritual state? Jesus teaches us to be wary of self-justification. You can't always judge where you're at with God simply by how you feel. This is the paradox of heaven.

Every valley shall be raised up,
every mountain and hill made low;
the rough ground shall become level,
the rugged places a plain.

Isaiah 40:4

68

Love and faithfulness meet together;
righteousness and peace kiss each other.
Faithfulness springs forth from the earth,
and righteousness looks down from heaven.

Psalm 85:10-11

Psalm 85 offers a beautiful image of the intimacy of spiritual relationship that is possible between ourselves and the Lord. We see that our spiritual life is not a matter of propelling ourselves willfully towards God. Nor is the objective to passively wait for the Lord to channel His spirit through us. The psalmist tells us plainly that the ideal of spiritual life is a "meeting together" of two wills, joined in the beautiful freedom of an embrace. These two wills are personified as *love* and *faithfulness*. Like good lovers, they always meet each other half-way.

In these verses, God is also identified as *righteousness.* As we embrace righteousness, the result is peace. The psalmist likens it to a kiss—the gentle, intimacy of lovers. It is an expression, at its exquisite best, of two parties, each acting freely, as both giver and receiver.

We are told that this spiritual embrace is a longed-for event that is anticipated by heaven. *Righteousness,* looking down, searches for evidence of *faithfulness* springing forth, as God, like a father, runs to embrace His approaching son or daughter. What a joy it is that our faithfulness causes such delight in God.

69

And without faith it is impossible to please God.

Hebrews 11:6

Faith is hard to sustain. It competes with our perception of reality. It implies risk and it always threatens to reveal us as fools if we're wrong. The fact that faith depends so much on God and so little on us is, of course, the reason why it honours the Lord so.

St. Isaac the Syrian, a desert hermit in the 7th century, often heard the confession of other monks who were tempted to reconsider their initial decision to follow God's will. Then, as now, the option of following our own will rather than waiting on God was an attractive one.

In his *Aesthetical Homilies* St. Isaac counsels,

> If you truly have faith in the omnipotence of God and believe that he manages all your affairs, do not then employ human craftiness. The man who takes refuge in faith never employs, or is engaged in, ways and means.

Are we relying on our own means, or on God's? For people of faith there needn't be any distinction. Faith can provide us with such assurance that even the thought of informing God about your needs can seem unnecessary. As St. Isaac writes elsewhere,

> Those to whom the light of faith has dawned are no longer so audacious as to pray on behalf of themselves; nor do they entreat God, saying, "Give this to us," or "Take that from us." For at every moment, by the eyes of faith, they see the fatherly providence

which comes of the true Father: he who, more than all, has the power and might to help us in a measure superabundantly greater than anything we might ask, think or conceive.

Father Matta El-Meskeen (Matthew the Poor), a spiritual descendant of the desert fathers, writes about the competing realities between the vision of faith and that of reason. In his *Orthodox Prayer Life* he says, "Reliance on empirical reason hampers the work of faith and frustrates the acceptance of its effectiveness."

We all know that, naturally speaking, a man cannot walk on the water, move mountains, nor rebuke the wind and waves. But faith is not dissuaded by nature or its laws. An over-concern with such laws often scuttles our faith.

According to Father Matta, two realities, fear and faith, always compete for the truth of how we interpret our situation. As he writes, "natural reason and calculation often foster fear, and fear leaves no room for faith." Fear he adds, is the most alienated point from God.

Faith is difficult to sustain, especially in times of trial and it is natural for all of us to waver in our resolve. St. Isaac prescribes an ongoing dialogue with the soul as the best remedy for fear.

> If once you have set your faith in the Lord, who is himself suf-
> ficient for your protection and care, and if you are following after
> him, take no thought again of your fears, but say to your soul: "He
> suffices me for all, to Whom I have altogether committed myself.
> I am not here (i.e. I am absent from all earthly concerns) and He
> knows this.

It's important to remind ourselves that there always exists an alternative to fear—the reality of a world in which God is truly present and active for the good of all who love Him.

70

My prayer is not that you take them out of the world but that
you protect them from the evil one. They are not of the world,
even as I am not of it. Sanctify them by the truth; your word is

truth. As you sent me into the world, I have sent them into the world.

John 17:15-19

Most spiritually-minded people living in the city are probably like me—a bit of a hybrid. There's a part of me that is deeply rooted in a timeless spirituality, while another part seems so much a product of this world. Being an enigma is one of the hazards of trying to live the spiritual life with a foot in two worlds. It splits you down the middle if you forget which side you come from.

As we read Jesus' words we are reminded once again of the mystery of our new origin. He sees us as *in* the world, but not *of* it. We come from somewhere else. It would make sense that only those who are "not of the world" can ever be "sent" to it. But it's a real challenge to keep that distinction in focus.

Let's not underestimate the forces that work against living a spiritual life in the city. Far easier to be in a monastery, on a retreat, or alone in the middle of creation. One of the reasons the early monks set out to live in the desert was to flee the confusion of the city. If the cities of the third century were too distracting for their spiritual focus what would they would make of our present-day treadmill?

Our contemporary life places unique demands on us, most of which have little to do with our spiritual needs. The way we plan our day, the environment in which we raise our children, the things we do in order to stay afloat in the city, all call for a different application of life than any of us would likely choose for ourselves. And the result is that we often feel disoriented, with a particular weariness that quenches our spiritual vitality. It can feel like you're only holding onto faith by a thread.

Being in the world is certainly a challenge. But this is where we belong, even if it goes against the grain of being a spiritual person. The Lord has placed us here, in a world where His light is easily obscured. And for the sake of those around us it's important that we learn how to keep our torches lit.

How do we do this? How do we remain credible as spiritual men and women? What boundaries are needed between us and the seemingly endless demands of contemporary life? What type of rule do we need in our lives to ensure that we are not being tossed to and fro by every wave of life-option?

Even in their times, Augustine, Benedict, Bernard and Francis recognized the necessity of having a "rule of life" in order to remain rooted in God. Whether living the cloistered life, or that of a free mendicant, a rule of life was seen as essential to prevent waywardness or dissipation of the soul. What about us? What would such a rule of life look like? What template would you provide for your day, your week or your year that would ensure you don't stray from your spiritual calling and formation?

These are important questions to ask ourselves. As a community of faith committed to spiritual growth we need to consider our way of life in order to remain fruitful in our goals—to protect God's investment in us, and to ensure our faithful response to the things He has already shown us.

The world needs contemplatives deep within the fabric of its cities, not only on the outskirts of its walls. It is the Lord who has called us here, and there is surely a special grace for those who pursue God in the confusion of urban life. Let us learn to do this well. And let us be careful to not lose the distinction between being *in* the world, and *of* it. This was Jesus' prayer for us.

The world is now in dire need of a living witness of faith issuing from a soul that has a true relationship with God. Such a witness out-weighs and outshines a thousand books on doctrine, faith, or prayer.

—Matthew the Poor

71

. . . He restores my soul.

Psalm 23:3

A farmer can't make a plant increase in size any more than a mother can cause her baby to grow. But both can contribute to an environment where growth is likely. Progress in the spiritual life, as well, is natural when an environment conducive for growth is present. There is no need to push forward in your faith, nor to pull yourself up by the bootstraps if you are in a healthy state of soul. Growth comes as naturally then as it does for a healthy baby.

The call to prayer is a God-given invitation for our souls to come and be restored to a condition that is optimum for spiritual growth. We experience the greatest sense of joy and fulfillment when we are in such a state of health. But there are many times in life when we are not thriving as we could. In the course of our days and weeks, our souls sometimes become ill, contaminated by deception, disappointment or fear. We lose our appetites, or we feel spiritually nauseous from something unhealthy that our hearts have ingested. Like all things in life, our spiritual health frequently needs to be restored before growth can continue.

One of the best prescriptions for someone who is ill is to simply rest— to allow the body time to re-gather its strength. For some sicknesses, fasting is also a natural remedy. The body instinctively knows that it doesn't want to eat, but needs to focus its energies on what ails. The inclination to withdraw and to sequester, which is so natural to the body, is also an instinct of the soul. Whenever it is in need of healing, our soul naturally desires to withdraw to a quiet place where it will not be taxed by any concerns other than its own restoration. We have all felt the need for such remedy at times.

To come to God often for the restoration of our spirits is simply good health care. It keeps us fresh, and in the optimum state for continuing growth. To recognize when you are ailing, and to be wise in doing something about it, will automatically bear good fruit in your life. As we are attentive to keeping our spirits restored, the progress of our souls will be the natural outcome.

72

Holy, holy, holy is the Lord of Hosts. The whole earth is full of your glory

Isaiah 6:3

These are the words Isaiah heard being prayed before the throne of God. It is a prayer recognizing that all of creation is filled with God's glorious Presence. And it is to the praise of this truth that a growing spiritual life inevitably leads us. With eyes wide-opened to the face of God, the automatic response of our souls will one day be awe at the evidence of the Lord's Presence, reflected in everything we see. The veil will be lifted. We will recognize the glory that has previously been hidden from view. And hearts, made pure by the grace of Christ, will see God as He is. This is the inevitable destination of our long spiritual journey. It's good to keep this in mind in the context of our day-to-day lives.

Most of our pursuit of God is naturally rooted in our temporal concerns. Where am I going? What should I do? How do I get this, or avoid that in my life? But even on earth, people who practice prayer notice a significant shift in focus that matures in them. The ultimate question changes from 'where is God in my life?' to 'where am I in God's life?' It is this shift in emphasis that prepares us for the glory of eternal prayer.

Matthew the Poor writes in his *Orthodox Prayer Life*,

> If we restrict prayer to the satisfaction of our needs and demands, or to responding to our pleas in this life, it loses its essential greatness. Through hallowing the name of God, paying homage to him, thanking and honouring him with pure praise, a person is transformed into a spiritual being. They thus join the heavenly host in their transcendent ministry.

Referring to this Isaiah passage he adds, "in its truest essence, prayer is a communion with the heavenly host in praising their Creator."

God certainly invites us to seek and find Him in our day-to-day experience. Signs of His participation in our lives are necessary assurances in our pilgrimage. But ultimately, it is the act of recognizing eternity in this life that joins us to heaven's praise. Every time our hearts are lifted in recognition of God's Presence we participate with the song sung by the already existing choirs of heaven. Some day soon we too will join them in full awareness of the Lord's majesty. We will be captivated by the beauty and glory of God that fills heaven and earth. And with senses wide-opened, our souls will respond with the only words appropriate to such an experience: "Holy, holy, holy...."

73

The LORD had said to Abram, "Leave your country, your people and your father's household and go to the land I will show you."

Genesis 12:1

We each carry within us visions of a promised land. Perhaps it's a life hope, or maybe just a short-term goal, or a circumstance we are hoping will better our lot in life. How we carry that hope within us is a matter that is determined by the particular character of our faith.

Faith is a subtle disposition that balances uncertainty along with realistic hope. It suggests a grace-sustained poise—a confidence that the One who makes promises will surely fulfill them. As it was with Abraham, the power of a promise goes a long way to refining our relationship with God.

Hope itself is not faith. By definition, it is more outward looking. It leans towards the future. Faith, on the other hand, is secure in the present for the simple reason that it feels secure about the future. Where hope is related to a desired outcome, faith finds rest in spite of the uncertainty as to how a promise will be fulfilled.

Abraham was called to leave the familiarity of his homeland. The only directions God gave him were to "go to the land I will show you." Only the Lord knew Abraham's eventual destination, and only He could reveal to him the time of his arrival. It would be natural for such uncertain conditions to create anxiety in most of us. If I were Abraham in this situation, I know my mind would be trying hard to second-guess God. Every oasis I stopped at would raise the question, "is this it?" Every word from a stranger about a land that lay ahead would cause me to entertain that the end of my journey was just over the next sand hill. Are we there yet? We don't get the sense that this was the character of Abraham's faith. He seemed much more poised, confident in spite of the uncertain ways God was leading him.

As I have watched myself at times when I have had a particular hope in God, I have observed many shades of character in my faith disposition. There are times when I must confess that my hope has been an anxious one. And yet there have been other times when I know it was poised securely in faith. This, I believe, is what Abraham was commended for.

The quality of Abraham's faith doesn't strike us as an anxious one. His confidence in the security of God's provision for him was what was credited to him as righteousness. It is obviously a very pleasing quality in the eyes of God, our Provider.

There is no occasion for tumult, strain, conflict, anxiety, once we have reached the living conviction that God is All. All takes place within Him. He alone matters.

—Evelyn Underhill

74

So now, go. I am sending you to Pharaoh to bring my people the Israelites out of Egypt." But Moses said to God, "Who am I, that I should go to Pharaoh and bring the Israelites out of Egypt?" And God said, "I will be with you.

Exodus 3:10-12

On the occasion of his conversion, it is said that St. Francis of Assisi wrestled all night in prayer with two simple questions: "who am I," and "who are You?" The answer he received to these questions dramatically altered his perspective and caused him to fearlessly commit the rest of his life to the God to whom he had prayed.

Moses as well, asks an important "who am I" question. The Lord has called him to a task and Moses' immediate response is one of questioning the wisdom of God's choice. There is an apparent disagreement between God and Moses as to who Moses really is. But the Lord's answer to Moses' question is an unexpected one.

If someone came to me with self-doubt my immediate response might be to assume they needed affirmation. I would consider ways to bolster their confidence with regards to the task ahead. But God takes a different tack with Moses. To the question "who am I?," the Lord responds with an oblique statement that seems to bypass Moses' query. "I will be with you."

How often do we feel similar self-doubts in our lives? *Who am I that I should be in such a ministry? Who am I that I should presume the love of my brothers and sisters? Who am I to think that God has purpose for me?* There are many ways that we could go about assuring ourselves, or one another, in the face of such doubts. *You can do it. You've got what it takes. It'll all work out somehow.* But God's word to us here seems quite different from the usual assurances we think we need. He simply states a fact of life that is meant to overarch all our doubts and fears: "I am with you." This, the Lord assumes, is all the information we need to muster the courage to obey.

It is good to consider in our own lives how God's assurance that "I am with you" represents the answer to all our "who am I?" questions. The Lord seems to think that this reply should be sufficient for our needs—that it will make a world of difference to your identity, your vocation, your future, your past, to be simply reminded that He is surely with you.

Surely I am with you always, to the very end of the age.
Matthew 28:20

RECOMMENDATIONS FOR CULTIVATING THE SPIRITUAL LIFE

Make every effort to add to your faith, . . . for if you possess these qualities in increasing measure, they will keep you from being ineffective and unproductive in your knowledge of our Lord Jesus Christ.

2 Peter 1:5-8

In an attempt to explore some basic disciplines that would contribute to spiritual goals I have listed a few "Rules of Life" below for us to consider. You will undoubtedly find that some of these "rules" are already a part of your Christian life. But consider others you might add as a way of cultivating your intentional relationship with God. The benefit in any of these comes primarily from establishing regular practices of our faith.

The phrase, "as you can," which precedes each rule suggests that you should freely accept the limitations of your life at this time. These limitations are unique to each one of us, as are the various seasons of our lives. Some of the natural constraints you feel might be related to your outside circumstances (i.e., busy schedules, too many other people around, an unconducive environment, etc.). Others will be related to the circumstances of your inner life (i.e., weariness, distractions of thought, anxiety, etc.).

The rules are divided into two sections: general (ongoing) and particular (daily). Let us consider how they might contribute to the overall quality of our spiritual life.

GENERAL RULES OF LIFE

As you can, meet regularly with a small group of people who know and share your deepest desires for relationship with God. Enjoy prayer together, communion, meditations on Scripture, and worship. Share your experiences of the journey of faith as you commit to encourage each other in your spiritual longings.

As you can, find a regular outlet through which to offer your time, money or labour for the sake of others. Volunteer to serve with a mission or some other help group. Visit the sick, care for the poor, remember the elderly and befriend those around you who are incapacitated in any way.

As you can, live a simple and uncluttered life. Have time for hospitality with everyone you meet in your day, especially God. Invite others into your life, your home, your journey.

As you can, meet regularly with a spiritual director or a friend who can help you remain objective about your spiritual life. Be cautious about overly assessing your sense of spiritual progress, or setbacks, on your own.

As you can, continually equip yourself for the sake of others. Learn new skills or perfect the gifts you have so that others may be blessed by them. Study and be eager to learn so that others may benefit. Endeavour to walk each day as close to God as possible so that the integrity of your spiritual life will encourage this in others as well.

As you can, plan dedicated times for spiritual retreat throughout the year—a day, a weekend, a week or more, away in silence with God. If you are married, help your spouse get away for times of renewal and recovery of spiritual focus.

PARTICULAR RULES OF LIFE

As you can, start each morning thanking God for all that will happen in the day ahead. Anticipate goodness and the Lord's love for you in all that will take place. Seek the Lord's purpose in every event as He works in and through you for the sake of salvation.

As you can, start each day with 20-30 minutes of silent prayer, remembering the ground of who you are, and of who God is in your life. Do this as a way of preparing the disposition of your heart before you apply yourself to your day. The quality you bring to your day will determine your effectiveness within it—how you respond, how you interpret, and how you contribute to the events of the day.

As you can, recall throughout the day one of the petitions of the Lord's Prayer (see meditation #27). Let the unique character of each of these prayers impress itself deeply on the character of your day.

As you can, practice Lectio Divina each day—a time of slow spiritual reading and study that has as its purpose the conversion of the heart more than the accumulation of the intellect. Read a short passage of Scripture, or from your own collection of spiritual wisdom you have gathered from others (if you don't have such a journal, begin one). Let this wisdom enter deeply as the foundation of your life.

As you can, take 5 minutes between the prolonged activities of your day to recollect your soul before God. Let times of rest be among the many activities of your day.

As you can, in the evening, spend another 20-30 minutes in silence before God. Recollect your day, especially noting times of spiritual enthusiasm or of spiritual difficulty (see meditation #39). Try to learn, from what God reveals to you in these times, how to adjust your life accordingly.

As you can, end each day in gratitude for all that has happened—for what has been given to you, and for what God has given to the world through your life, your thoughts, your prayers. Be grateful for the simple fact of life and for the invitation you have to play a constructive part in the incredible story of Christ's presence unfolding.

BIBLIOGRAPHY
OF WORKS CITED

St. John of the Cross, *The Dark Night of the Soul* (London: Hodder & Stoughton, 1988).

Richard Rohr, Everything Belongs (New York: Crossroad Publishing, 1999).

Jeanne Guyon, *Experiencing the Depths of Jesus Christ* (Auburn Maine: Christian Books Publishing House, 1975).

Teresa of Avila, *A Life of Prayer*. Classics of Faith and Devotion. Series, ed. James Houston (Vancouver, B.C.: Regent College Publishing, 1998).

Abbé de Tourville, *Letters of Direction* (London: Mowbray, 1982).

Matthew the Poor, *Orthodox Prayer Life* (Crestwood, NY: St. Vladimir's Seminary Press, 2003).

Simon Tugwell, *Prayer in Practice* (Springfield, Ill.: Templegate Publ., 1974).

Evelyn Underhill, *The Spiritual Life* (Harrisburg, Penn. Morehouse, 1937).

Albert Haase, O.F.M, *Swimming in the Sun* Cincinnati, Ohio: St. Anthony Messenger Press, 1993).

François Fénélon, *Talking with God* (Brewster, Mass.: Paraclete Press, 1997).

Ronald Rolheiser, *The Shattered Lantern* (New York: Crossroad Pub., 2001).

St. Francis de Sales, *Thy Will Be Done* (Manchester, N.H.: Sophia Press, 1995).

James M. Houston, *The Transforming Power of Prayer* (Colorado Springs, Co.: Navpress, 1996).

SCRIPTURE INDEX

Printed in the United States
145608LV00009B/41/A